THE CULTURE OF SELFLESSNESS

The first Christian doctors: Cosmas and Damian
Cathedral, Essen, Germany. (Photo by Sophia van Dijk)

THE CULTURE OF SELFLESSNESS

Rudolf Steiner, the Fifth Gospel,
and the Time of Extremes

PETER SELG

2012
STEINERBOOKS

SteinerBooks
610 Main Street, Great Barrington, MA 01230
www.steinerbooks.org

Translated by Catherine E. Creeger

Originally published in German as *Die Kultur der Selbstlosigkeit.
Rudolf Steiner, das Fünfte Evangelium und das Zeitalter der Extreme* by
Verlag am Goetheanum, Dornach, Switzerland 2006. www.VamG.ch

Library of Congress Cataloging-in-Publication Data is available.

ISBN: 978-1-62148-011-2

Contents

Preface

> We must first become selfless in our ethics, in our
> understanding of the world, and in our consciousness
> soul activity. As contemporary culture moves toward
> the future, one of its tasks is for humanity to become
> ever more selfless. Herein lies the future of real ethical
> activity in life, of loving deeds that can be performed by
> humanity on earth. — Rudolf Steiner (GA 152, 151ff.[1])

IN A LECTURE held in Basel on June 1, 1914, eight weeks before
the outbreak of World War I, Rudolf Steiner, conscious of developments to come, coined the phrase "culture of selflessness" to
describe the culture that would develop in the future. The far-
reaching social implications of his primarily Christological lectures on the Fifth Gospel, given in 1913/14 under the same political circumstances, were foreign to many of Steiner's contemporary audiences, who largely failed to understand his dramatic
accounts drawn from the Fifth Gospel (or that gospel itself) as a
"source of comfort" for the future, or (as Rudolf Steiner said of
them) as "needed" for future work. The subsequent catastrophes
of the twentieth and early twenty-first centuries, however, have
sensitized us to Steiner's central themes and contents of 1913/14.
He spoke then of spiritual development and self-preservation in
the face of great suffering, of truly participating in the misfor-
tunes of others, and of acquiring "true selflessness" that takes the
human "I" fully into account.

During the 1930s, during the National Socialist reign of
violence, a few of Rudolf Steiner's students took this path of moral
resistance and all-embracing therapeutic action. One example is

described in the second chapter of this volume. Many other destinies are less well known; by now, they can no longer be completely
saved from oblivion. They include the great life work of Maria
Krehbiel-Darmstädter, an anthroposophist of Jewish origin who
was murdered in Auschwitz in January 1943.[2] But both now and
in the future, in a world that must find humane ways to endure
continued calamities of tremendous magnitude, the task Rudolf
Steiner described remains relevant in all cultures and all parts of
the globe. "A single great community covers the earth. Its name
is suffering and strength." (Krehbiel-Darmstädter).[3]

The themes developed in this book were initially presented
in lecture form at the Christmas Conference of the General
Anthroposophical Society on December 29, 2005. With that
context in mind, I ended the preface to the first edition with
these sentences, which are still valid: "My personal thanks go
out to my friend Sergei O. Prokofieff, not only for his invita-
tion to lecture at the Christmas Conference, but even more for
his significant spiritual-scientific activity. Since 1982, he has been
shedding light on Rudolf Steiner's work from the Christological
perspective, and making it accessible in extensive publications
that elaborate on many of the themes in this book."

PETER SELG

Director of the Ita Wegman Institute
for Basic Research into Anthroposophy

Arlesheim, November 2010

Introduction

> Taken together, the effect was like a thunderclap,
> like awakening from deep sleep. (Andrei Belyi)[4]

RUDOLF STEINER'S LECTURES on the Fifth Gospel took place in the context of the immediate pre-war period—the time "before 1914," which was rapidly drawing to a close. They were given in the last few months of 1913, during the dawning of catastrophic developments that would define the history of the twentieth century, and would persist even today in many of their characteristic features. The war that began in the summer of 1914 not only brought the end of "yesterday's world," the old European order, but was also the first war to affect major portions of humanity. While the Austrian playwright and journalist Karl Kraus was writing his epic documentary drama, "The Last Days of Humanity" in Vienna, all of the major powers of the time and all of the nations of Europe (with the exception of Spain, the Netherlands, the Scandinavian countries, and Switzerland) were going to war; a war that would see not only American combat troops in Europe, but also armies from Australia and New Zealand in the Aegean for the first time. That war would ultimately kill eight million people and wound twenty-one million. Thus the First World War marked the beginning of an "age of extremes."[5] The seemingly apocalyptic twentieth century, in which the European continent or the "Christian West" irrevocably lost its leading role in history, was characterized by a cascade of previously unimaginable destruction affecting all of civilization—the culmination of egomaniacal technological forces in the service of doom.

"The threat of war is constant," Rudolf Steiner wrote to his mother in spring of 1913, seven months before beginning his lectures in Kristiania (now Oslo) (34, 455). In Dornach, Rudolf Steiner was urgently attempting to make the completion of the Goetheanum a reality; on the construction site, his repeated challenges to awaken were becoming familiar:

> How often we saw Dr. Steiner going from one person to the next uttering the simple words, "There will be war; it is going to be terrible." It was as if he was waiting for something, and we could hardly bear to look at him. "Yes, Herr Doktor, it does look as if war is coming." And he went away, as if disappointed. "Only forty people wanted it to happen," he said when the war broke out, "and there were too few who didn't want it." (Assya Turgenieff)[6]

On June 29, 1914, the painter Herman Linde brought Rudolf Steiner the news of the assassination in Sarajevo, which would lead to the beginning of the war four weeks later. Linde and several other bystanders experienced Steiner's immediate reaction:

> I will never forget the expression on Rudolf Steiner's face at that moment. His eyes were wide open and filled with immense horror and sadness as he spoke the words, "Now the catastrophe is closing in." (Hilde Boos-Hamburger)[7]

> Dr. Steiner's expression was as shattered as if he had been struck by lightning; we scarcely dared to look at him. He was silent, looking at us as if attempting to read our faces for what we had heard of the event. Abruptly, he asked a few people "Have you read about the assassination in Sarajevo?" To us, it was an exciting event; to him, the catastrophe in its full scope. But he said nothing. (Natalie Turgenieff-Pozzo)[8]

*

The lecture cycle Rudolf Steiner began in Oslo on October 1, 1913, was not a direct response to imminent historical and political events, yet the connection cannot be overlooked. Although these lectures expanded on a Jesus-centered Christology, Steiner placed more emphasis on the processes of soul and spirit it was meant to elicit, and he did so in the context of a striking contemporary situation to which he referred repeatedly: "Now humanity must begin to grasp contemporary events consciously. This is why humanity must get to know Christ even better, and understanding the person of Jesus of Nazareth is part of knowing Christ" (148, 219).

Rudolf Steiner also pointed out repeatedly and explicitly that accounts from the Fifth Gospel were especially important "in relationship to modern times and current circumstances" (148, 9). As he said on November 4, 1913, in Berlin, the "spiritual powers of our time" were demanding "that from now on, a number of souls know about these things," "a small number of souls" (148, 134, and 323).

> And as difficult as it may be to speak of these matters without holding back, especially at present, there remains a real obligation to give individual souls what they will increasingly need to develop toward the future (148, 154) ... Despite any personal inclination to avoid speaking of them, they will be communicated out of an inner sense of obligation for as long as they can be told to human souls. They will be needed in humanity's evolution. The souls who receive them now will certainly need them for work that will have to be done on the level of soul and spirit in the course of humanity's further evolution. (148, 324)

In many similar passages, Rudolf Steiner referred repeatedly to the preparatory character of the contents he drew from events at the beginning of the Christian era, contents that he expected his audience to relive inwardly. In the souls of his listeners, these contents were meant to serve something "that must be prepared" for the future. The contemporary civilized world was characterized by an accretion of soon-to-be-discharged destructive forces catastrophic to humanity, and its Christian or Christological consciousness was headed for complete dissolution.[9] Against this background, in ways never heard before, Rudolf Steiner revealed contents diametrically opposed to the dynamics of evil, contents resounding with the future-bearing sacrificial substance of true selflessness:

> Taken together, the effect was like a thunderclap, like awakening from deep sleep. (Andrei Belyi)[10]

*

1

The Fifth Gospel

Human beings will have to trade the spirit of mere thinking for the spirit of directly beholding, sensing, and experiencing the spiritual, living Christ who accompanies all human souls.

— RUDOLF STEINER (GA 152, 92)

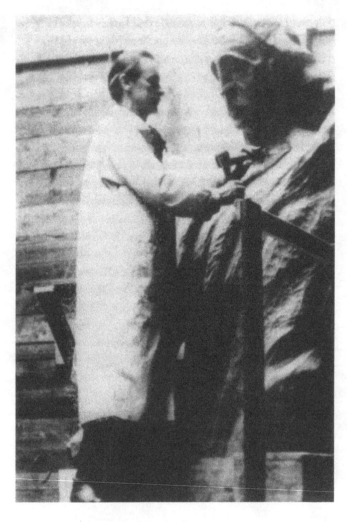

Rudolf Steiner at work on the figure of Christ
Dornach, 1916

IN SPITE OF their very differentiated and varied contents, Rudolf Steiner's presentations of the Fifth Gospel all reveal a single central motif—that of selfless devotion and freely chosen self-sacrifice.

Rudolf Steiner tells us that because Jesus of Nazareth shared in the suffering of all of humanity, the path of development that led to the baptism in the Jordan was already characterized by unspeakable suffering. From the beginning, Jesus' path was determined by the greatest possible empathy. Rudolf Steiner called the Luke Jesus a "genius of the heart," possessed of an exceptional capacity for love and empathy: "Since earliest childhood, he had shown himself to be especially gifted at putting himself in the place of others, in feeling their suffering and joy as his own suffering and joy. He possessed this ability to the greatest possible extent" (148, 285).

After the "transposition of the 'I'" experienced by Jesus of Nazareth at age twelve (that is, after his union with the Zarathustra being), his entire development as a child, adolescent, and adult stood under the sign of great "despair at the fate of earthly humanity" (148, 255). As time went on, he increasingly experienced and perceived humanity's spiritual fall, which held great cultural consequences for civilization, and led individuals astray in illness and despair—processes that Jesus of Nazareth perceived deeply and experienced empathetically: "Jesus of Nazareth had become someone who saw more deeply into life's mysteries than anyone else on earth had yet been able to do. More than anyone else, he was able to observe the full extent to which human misery can be intensified" (148, 66).

In his lectures on the Fifth Gospel, Rudolf Steiner described such situations in detail and spoke of the "infinite suffering" of Jesus of Nazareth: "We see his infinite suffering, which cannot compare to any suffering on earth" (148, 134). This infinite suffering or compassion also led him to wonder whether humanity might be redeemed by a new spiritual impulse "of profound and elemental power" (148, 71). Rudolf Steiner tells us that all of the soul processes associated with Jesus' empathy were shaped by far-reaching selflessness and ultimately made possible the Christ Event of the baptism in the Jordan; that is, Jesus' longed-for "macrocosmic illumination of the earth" (148, 298). It took the form of Christ's becoming human, which would reverse humanity's decline and transform it into a new spiritual ascent.

At the same time, however, Christ Jesus' path after the baptism was also essentially a path of suffering, brought about by the destinies of others. In Oslo on October 6, 1913, Rudolf Steiner spoke of Christ Jesus' wanderings after the triple temptation, and his encounters and experiences with people who lived "on bread alone":

> He *felt* the entirety of human incarnation in the physical world. He *felt* how in humanity's evolution, the need to incarnate had gone so far that physical incarnation led people to forget the names of the fathers in the heavens, the names of the spirits of the higher hierarchies. And he *felt* how there were no longer any people who could hear the voices of the prophets of old and the message of Zarathustra's wisdom. Now he *knew* that living on daily bread is what separates human beings from the heavens. It drives them to egotism and inevitably leads them into Ahriman's clutches. (148, 91; italics added).

Again his cognition ("now he *knew*") developed through empathetic suffering, through feeling and empathizing with the situation of others. In Christ Jesus, the transformed voice of the Bath Kol, perceived years earlier by Jesus of Nazareth with the "macrocosmic Our Father" in all of its implications for humanity, became a reality, along with the full scope of the third (ahrimanic) temptation.[11] He then set out to complete the process of an incarnation that would ultimately become absolute; that is, his complete, freely willed penetration of the physical nature of Jesus. He endured "being pressed into its three bodies" (148, 277), freely accepting this burden as a means of imbuing earthly processes with the Christ essence in the struggle with Ahriman. The resulting suffering, which "transcends all human ability to conceive of suffering" (148, 277), became the hallmark of his path to Golgotha.

*

On October 1, 1913, Rudolf Steiner began depicting the stages of Christ's earthly incarnation with full intensity. Then, in Leipzig on December 30, 1913, on the next-to-last day of the year before the war, he began describing the sacrifices of the Christ Being prior to earthly life as Christ Jesus. Until the early summer of 1914, Steiner devoted further lectures to this subject, focusing not only on the Christ Being, but also on the being of the child Jesus of Luke's Gospel, who entered earthly incarnation for the first time at the beginning of the first Christian millennium. As the "sister soul" of Adam, this Nathan being had dwelt in cosmic heights, where it remained untouched and uninfluenced by all of the adversarial forces' intrusions and temptations that characterized humanity's evolution on earth. Nonetheless, this soul experienced human beings' tragic situation three times during the earth's Lemurian and Atlantean evolutionary epochs. According to Rudolf Steiner's account, during these epochs luciferic and ahrimanic demons took possession of the earthly human constitution, which tended to result in the separation of the spirit-soul's incarnation structures (and in certain respects even the spirit-soul itself). These demons imbued human physical, etheric, and soul processes with toxic selfishness, corrupting them in ways both dramatic and tragic. In cosmic heights, the Nathan being not only perceived the resulting suffering but internalized it with empathy and responded with self-sacrifice:

We are dealing here with a superhuman entity, a being who lived in the spiritual world and heard humanity crying out in misery, calling out to the spiritual worlds for help. This being prepared to receive the Christ Being (149, 49). ...Humanity cried out in pain and torment, and its cries rose up to that spirit being, who responded by seeking permission from the Sun Spirit to become imbued with the Christ (152, 94).

Deep within, the Nathan soul sensed the tragedy of humanity's evolution (148, 53). This archangel-like being sacrificed its soul to the Christ Being in three successive stages. Rudolf Steiner continues, telling us that the Christ Being accepted this sacrifice and spiritualized the proffered soul body; that is, the Christ Being assumed soul form in the Nathan being in a parallel threefold act of sacrifice. Steiner tells us that the three stages of this cosmic process took place in the sun sphere, in planetary space, and in the environs of the planets close to the earth.[12] The Christ-imbued Nathan being was then able to "radiate strength into the earth's aura" (152, 123); rays of strength that reached the physical, etheric, and soul aspects of the human constitution, re-stabilizing their internal organization and imbuing them with selflessness. Before this sacrificial intervention took place, the human senses had retreated into self-centered hypersensitivity. Human life functions and organs had become increasingly isolated and autonomous, with pathological consequences for the human constitution as a whole. "Illness means that an organ has become self-serving and is leading a life of its own within the body" (152, 156). Human soul forces had become independent of and dissociated from each other. Through Christ's three sacrifices prior to the beginning of the Christian era, human nature was harmoniously restructured and made spiritually receptive on the physical, etheric, and astral levels:

The senses said: Not I, but Christ in us.
The life organs said: Not I, but Christ in us.
The organs of feeling said: Not I, but Christ in us. (152, 163)

The three sacrifices by the Christ Being (and the Nathan being) thus created the physiological prerequisites for events at the turn of the millennium to take effect; that is, for processes of self-lessness on the level of the "I" that had now become necessary: "Human moral and intellectual activity must learn to say: Not I, but Christ in me." (152, 163).

The Nathan being's empathetic suffering at the hand of human-ity's fate had become the prerequisite for that being's threefold permeation by the Christ, and for the salvation of the human constitution during the early stages of Earth evolution. In turn, the selfless, empathetic path of Jesus of Nazareth, in whom the Nathan being incarnated on earth for the first time, then pro-vided the prerequisite for this fourth-stage Christ; that is, for the baptism in the Jordan, which was to make possible the indepen-dent and selfless evolution of the human "I." "Human moral and intellectual activity must learn to say: Not I, but Christ in me." (152,163).

*

As Rudolf Steiner indicated in various passages in his lectures on the Fifth Gospel, the primary purpose of his accounts was to allow his listeners' souls to trace the path of suffering of Jesus of Nazareth, especially as it led up to the baptism in the Jordan:

> The point is to develop a living feeling for what Jesus' soul underwent in the experiences I have described, to feel the infinite pain of his loneliness. It is not so important to be able to recount (either to yourself or to others) the events I have attempted to describe here. Rather, you will under-stand something of the significance of Jesus' experiences in preparation for the Mystery of Golgotha only if you can imagine what this human being, Jesus of Nazareth, had to suffer before he could approach the Mystery of Golgotha so that the Christ Impulse could flow into earthly evolution.

> Your soul must be profoundly moved, even shattered, by
> tracing this suffering. (148, 310ff.)

Rudolf Steiner emphasizes the importance of acquiring a "living sense" of Jesus' path of suffering and sacrifice, a "sensed concept" (152, 75) or "living imagination" that moves and shatters
human souls until they are ultimately capable of experiencing the
possibility and the reality of the Christ Impulse for themselves:

> We can evoke a living imagination of this Christ Impulse by
> reawakening Christ's suffering in ourselves, by reviewing
> the details of his life and attempting to call up the corre-
> sponding emotions. The more we succeed in evoking the
> weaving, surging emotions of a being like Jesus of Nazareth,
> the more deeply we penetrate such mysteries. (148, 310ff.)

> To grasp the greatest of all things, the ultimate in soul
> exertion is required in order to achieve the inner intensity
> of feeling and sensing that is needed if the sublime is to
> approach our souls to some extent. (142,121)

Thanks to Rudolf Steiner's accounts from the Fifth Gospel, calling to mind Jesus' feelings before the baptismal event is now a
concrete possibility. For Steiner, this was the first step in a process
of soul preparation and transformation that would ultimately lead
not only to understanding the Christ Impulse, but also to realizing it in the Pauline sense. In Dornach on October 6, 1921, seven
years after ending his lectures on the Fifth Gospel, Rudolf Steiner
responded to a question from Constantin Neuhaus, a priest of the
Old Catholic Church, about striving to imitate Christ:

> The concept of *imitatio* includes transforming our feelings
> and our inner life so they resemble the life of Christ. The
> *imitatio Christi* should not be ruled out, but I prefer to
> speak of an *imitatio Jesu*, since of course it is possible to

become similar to Jesus in our human attributes. The similarity, however, ends with the final stages of the Mystery of Golgotha. Christians can become similar to Christ through the Christ's living in them in the Pauline sense. That is the appropriate Christian concept, and it can be understood only in the sense of Christ's becoming alive in us through his presence. When individuals become Christ-like, they do so through the Pauline "Christ in me." (343, 450)

*

Inasmuch as Rudolf Steiner repeatedly emphasized the *preparatory* character of his lectures on the Fifth Gospel, the far-reaching Pauline dimension of their focus must be taken into account.[13] At the same time, however, these lectures must clearly also be seen in the narrower context of Steiner's explanations of the future coming of the Christ Being in the etheric; that is, of the increasing possibility of experiencing the Christ Being etherically. As Steiner had explained repeatedly since 1908, theosophic or anthroposophic spiritual-scientific training was specifically intended as preparation for this event:

> We learn that [theosophic-anthroposophic spiritual science] imposes a tremendous responsibility on us, because it is preparation for the concrete event of the reappearance of Christ. Christ will reappear because human beings rise to meet him through etheric vision. Having understood this, we see spiritual science as preparing human beings for Christ's reappearance. (118, 28)

Rudolf Steiner's lectures on the Fifth Gospel dealt consistently with events at the beginning of the Christian era, as preserved in the cosmic chronicle of "akashic substance." Steiner clearly strove to enable his listeners to "reawaken" or "remember" these events in soul and spirit, especially with regard to the path of selflessness that led Jesus to the event at the Jordan. On the other hand, Steiner's lectures were firmly grounded in the present and future, and they served as preparation for events yet to come or already partially present. In Copenhagen on October 14, 1913, Rudolf Steiner explicitly linked these two themes: "Human beings will have to trade the spirit of mere thinking for the spirit of directly beholding, sensing, and experiencing the spiritual living Christ who accompanies all human souls" (152, 92).

Five months earlier, in London, he had said: "Beginning in the twentieth century, the life of Christ will increasingly become a matter of direct personal experience for human souls" (152, 46).

Rudolf Steiner clearly related this direct personal experience to the "intentions of the *living Christ*" (262, 26) as they can be experienced now, and will be experienced in the future, as well as to etheric encounters with the Christ Being. "Directly sensing and experiencing," however, also meant methodically and precisely calling to mind the three years, and events leading up to them. In other words, recollections in soul and spirit were the prerequisite to (or facilitator of) possible future encounters and connections. As Steiner explained in detail for the first time in a major lecture in Cologne on May 18, 1912, the reappearing earthly "sheaths" of the Christ spirit will be formed entirely of the soul-spiritual attitudes and work of human souls. These sheaths, which come about through human freedom, correspond to an astral, etheric, and physical "bodily nature" for the Christ Spirit. As such, they make it possible for the earth to be imbued by the Christ in successive stages. There can be no doubt that Rudolf Steiner's accounts from the Fifth Gospel were intended as preparation for the formation of these sheaths, especially on the central level of the etheric body. In Cologne, Rudolf Steiner provided details about the three types of forces necessary for developing the corresponding "bodies," saying, "All of these sheaths will take shape out of forces that humanity must develop on earth. What are those forces?"

As human beings stand in awe at the spiritual world's great revelations and truths, they imbue themselves with a feeling of *wonder* that gradually, over the ages, develops into a force of attraction for the Christ Impulse. As the Christ Spirit is drawn in, the Christ Impulse unites with individual human souls to the extent that they are capable of standing in awe of cosmic mysteries. The Christ's astral body in earthly evolution is derived from all the feelings of wonder that have lived in individual human souls.

The second attribute that human souls must develop to attract the Christ Impulse is the feeling of *compassion*. Whenever a feeling of compassion or shared joy develops in a human soul, it serves as a force of attraction for the Christ Impulse. Through compassion and love, Christ unites with human souls. Compassion and love are the forces from which the Christ will shape his own etheric body until the end of the Earth phase of evolution.

A third attribute that enters the human soul as if from a higher world is the *conscience* we obey, placing greater value on it than on our own individual moral instincts. Christ unites most intimately with conscience, deriving his physical body from impulses of conscience in individual human souls.

When we know that Christ's etheric body develops out of human feelings of compassion and love, the biblical statement, "What you have done to the least of my brothers, you have done to me," becomes very real indeed, because until the end of the Earth phase of evolution, Christ will shape his etheric body out of human compassion and love. (143, 183ff.)

*

Union with the Christ Being (as understood in the concrete Pauline sense, and characterized by a distinct quality of encounter) also stood at the center of the new mystery site of the first

Goetheanum. Looking back one year after its destruction by fire, Rudolf Steiner said:

> In Ephesus stood the statue of the goddess; but here in the Goetheanum stood the statue of the human being, the representative of humanity, Christ Jesus. In *identifying with him* in all due humility, our intention in placing it here is to be as completely absorbed in awareness of him as the pupils of Ephesus (in their own way, which humanity today can no longer completely understand) were absorbed in the Diana of Ephesus. (260, 248/250; italics added).

The Christ statue of the Goetheanum bears the imprint of the radiating forces of conscience, compassion, and wonder.[15] In other words, the "representative of humanity" appears in a form sculpted by those very forces and qualities of individuals and of humanity that must serve to fashion the sheaths of the coming Christ Impulse at present and in the future. Two thousand years ago, lengthy preparation involving the union of mystery streams was required for the Christ to become human, and the resulting body was then further transformed by the incarnating Christ. Now and in the future, the qualities that once lived in those mystery streams as the moral attitudes and actions of individual human souls must be created and made available to the (re)appearing Christ Spirit. To this end and on a higher level, Rudolf Steiner united the historical events of the beginning of the Christian era (that is, the *physical* incarnation and revelation of Christ: *"Yes, that is the Christ; that is how my spiritual eye beheld him"*)[16] and the impending "beginning of the cosmic era" with its *etheric* revelation of the Christ.

*

Rudolf Steiner understood the human being's "identification" with the "representative of humanity"—with the "spiritual, living Christ progressively moving [toward human beings] from

East to West," as it was intended and made possible in the first Goetheanum—as the future goal of the social development of human selflessness. Willem Zeylmans van Emmichoven put it this way, "The individual human 'I' is being prepared to become the bearer of humanity's 'I.' The human being is becoming humanity; humanity as a whole lives in the individual."[17] Rudolf Steiner described in detail in his lectures on the Fifth Gospel (148) and on the preliminary stages of the Mystery of Golgotha (152) that Jesus of Nazareth (and also Christ Jesus and the earlier Nathan being) not only experienced the "fate of earthly *humanity* with compassion, inwardly accompanying and supporting all of humanity's existence, but also encompassed the entire social context and the totality of all human souls.

The individual's path to Christ is now reversed with regard to humanity, allowing the individual "I" to offer itself up selflessly in the broadest sense, through Pauline enhancement (not negation) of its individual qualities.[18] Thus this path leads to an interim goal of one of the major evolutionary trends in the human organism; a development that leads human beings from our original unconscious selflessness (and existence within the cosmos) through an epoch of necessary selfishness and self-focus to "insightful selflessness." "Human beings must pass through selfishness in order to achieve selflessness on a higher, fully conscious level" (11, 63). This direction in humanity's evolution, which was and is initiated and carried by active Christ impulses (116, 66), determines the configuration and ongoing development of the human organization in relationship to body, soul, and spirit, right into concrete physiology. Among other things, it makes possible the development of selfless sensory perception that transcends the animal organism's self-centered bodily and environmental frame of reference.[19] It then also allows the birth of a specific "sense of ego"; that is, the ability to perceive the "I" of another human being. Rudolf Steiner tells us that this perception requires temporarily turning off one's own thinking while submitting completely to the thinking of the other person.[20] At least temporarily, it leads to "sensing another being and feeling at one with that being, sensing the other as oneself" (170, 110). Selflessness, which Rudolf Steiner described in an earlier work as the "feeling of sympathy among human beings" (99, 141), underlies the ability to intuit one's way into the "I" of the other person in the same way that developing and practicing intuitive perceptual capabilities enhances a person's "insightful selflessness":

> The more strongly we practice and develop this fully conscious devotion to the other being, the greater our selflessness becomes, and the greater our love for that being must be. In this way we feel the ability to live in another being instead of in ourselves; that is, to step out of our own being into that of another, becoming ever stronger. We achieve intuition, which means that we no longer experience only ourselves. Instead we learn to experience the other in complete selflessness while fully maintaining our individualization. (84, 231)

Rudolf Steiner tells us that in the type of self-experience accessible to us on a daily basis, the "true I" of one's own being is encountered as a "foreign being" and must therefore be discovered with the help of a higher "sense of ego" (84, 142).[21] As another form of intuitively active selflessness, this encounter implies a further enhancement of the activity of loving and is thus also the prerequisite to developing the future bodily nature of the human being in which selflessness will become a decisive sphere of formative forces. Steiner says that in future the Word (not the intrinsically egotistical sexual organs) will be capable of bringing forth human beings.[22] This type of reproduction will be associated with profound changes in the body's central cardiovascular system: "Selflessness will be transformed into an attribute of the blood, and the organ of thinking will shift into the heart" (96, 293). Even our physiology will reflect the advance of human selflessness. Because of the activity of the Christ Impulse, selflessness will evolve and unfold through the stages of (body-transcending) sensory perception; the sense of ego; and the experience of the "higher I" until it achieves the possibility of reproduction and incarnation.[23]

*

In other lectures, Rudolf Steiner explained further that, at present, the sphere of the etherized blood ascending from the heart to the head is capable of uniting with the etherized blood of Christ, which has maintained a connection to the earth since the event of Golgotha (Basel, October 1, 1911; GA 230). "Selflessness will be transformed into an attribute of the blood." Although possible, this union requires a modern understanding of the Christ Being as made possible by the Christology of modern spiritual science, including Steiner's communications from the Fifth Gospel on the life of Christ Jesus, which are intended to be followed with empathy. In turn, this understanding enables the union of the two blood streams, which forms the physiological basis for concrete perception of the Christ Being in the etheric. Thus Rudolf Steiner's "communications" from the Fifth Gospel were a significant preparatory stage in bringing about this future event, which is inextricably linked to the human moral development that leads to selflessness.[24, 25] In Leipzig on November 4, 1911, two years before beginning his lectures in Oslo, Rudolf Steiner said:

> The specific goal of the spiritual-scientific movement in our time is for human moral impulses to relate correctly to Christ. Christ is the actual moral impulse that imbues humanity with moral strength. The Christ Impulse is strength and life; it is the moral energy that pervades human beings. This moral energy, however, needs to be understood. For our time in particular, the presence of Christ needs to be proclaimed. That is anthroposophy's

task—to proclaim the presence of Christ in the etheric form. (130, 118ff.)

Rudolf Steiner speaks of two factors that will profoundly reshape human morality: the future (but already dawning) experience of "Christ in the etheric form"; and the fact that the active Christ Being is taking charge of human destiny.[26] If nothing else, said Steiner, the future culture of selflessness will be substantiated and determined by the reality of direct perception of the karmic consequences of our actions, in the form of anticipatory presentiments, or sensing the need to balance out some action:

> For example, to people who feel the urge to step back from what they have done, remarkable dream-like images will appear. They will see what appear to be actions they have taken, but they will not be able to remember having done what the image suggests. They will then know that the image appearing to their souls presages a karmic action they must take in the future, whether in this lifetime or the next, in order to balance out deeds in the past. In short, individuals will gradually acquire the ability to behold, as if in a dream, their future karmic compensatory actions. (130, 167)

In Karlsruhe on October 14, 1911, Rudolf Steiner explained this further:

> Humanity's next epoch will see the emergence of enhanced capabilities that will be closely linked to human experiences and will serve as powerful incentives to human morality. These incentives will mean something very different from their precursor, the voice of conscience. People will no longer believe that what they have done will die with them. They will know quite well that their actions will not die with them, but will have consequences that will continue to

live with them. This is one of the things people will know in the future. The time when the gates to the spiritual world were closed to human beings is coming to an end. (131, 216ff.)

At the same time, however, the Christ Being appearing in the etheric will provide ever-increasing support to individuals in difficult situations, decisions, and actions in life. Christ will be "visible to newly awakened human faculties, counseling and protecting individuals who need advice, help, or consolation in the loneliness of life":

There will come times when specific situations will make individuals feel sorrowful and miserable. Increasingly in these times to come, as the force of individuality in people's lives increases, one person's help for another will become less important and valuable. It will become less and less possible for one person to intervene helpfully in another person's soul, as happened quite readily in ancient times. Instead, however, the great Counselor will appear here and there as an etheric figure. (130, 168)

Christ will stand beside individuals and be their counselor. This is no mere image. In reality, people will receive the advice they need from the living Christ, who will be their counselor and friend. He will speak to human souls like a physical human being who accompanies us. (152, 91)

*

2

The Culture of Selflessness

For them at that time, Christ became a unique big brother who was always there with them, even closer than death.

— INGE SCHOLL,
sister of Hans and Sophie Scholl[27]

Hans Scholl, Sophie Scholl, Christoph Probst, summer 1942

In Basel on June 1, 1914 (eight weeks before the beginning of World War I was to set in motion an unimaginable dynamic of death, destruction, and devastation unprecedented in the history of humanity, made possible and supported by ahrimanic machines and technology), Rudolf Steiner said in his last lecture on the four sacrifices of Christ:

> Acknowledging the Christ means going through the school of selflessness.... Under the influence of materialism, selflessness was lost to humanity in a way that we will recognize only in times still to come. We can, however, regain a culture of selflessness by immersing ourselves in the Mystery of Golgotha on the level of feeling; by applying our entire soul being to the task. We can then say that what Christ did for earthly evolution is contained in the fundamental impulse of selflessness; and for the human soul's conscious evolution, Christ can become the school of selflessness.
>
> ...
>
> We must first become selfless in our ethics, in our understanding of the world, and in the activity of our consciousness soul. As contemporary culture moves toward the future, one of its tasks is for humanity to become ever more selfless. Herein lies the future of real ethical activity in life, of loving deeds that can be performed by earthly humanity. (152, 151ff.)

Two weeks after the beginning of the war, at a first aid course at the Goetheanum, Rudolf Steiner said, "It is certainly possible that some of us will be in a position to help others."[28] He gave the course together with a Ukrainian Jewish physician, Dr. Henrietta Ginda Fritken, who was later murdered in one of the National Socialist concentration camps. Together they not only explained first aid and bandaging techniques, but also spoke from spiritual and esoteric perspectives about the appropriate soul-spiritual attitude of first responders, and about the need to find one's way "into the helper's role with all one's soul and mind."[29] Rudolf Steiner emphasized the Pauline spirit of "not I, but Christ in me"; and he spoke of a comprehensive "ideal" that would be fully realized only in the future, but was already beginning to appear in therapeutic situations:

> Humanity will be fully present only when it becomes possible for one individual's pain to be felt not only by the person in question but also by anyone else....
>
> This is the ideal that still eludes us: In the future, the spiritual aspect of the human being will become so strong that the pain of a person with an injured body will be felt not only in that person's consciousness, but also equally keenly by others. Some day we will be able to feel another person's injury as acutely as if it were our own. That is the Christ ideal, and at times like this it is good to remember this ideal.[30]

Rudolf Steiner then formulated a mantra in support of those who might need to serve as first responders:

> Providing first aid is informed by the ideal contained in the following lines, which I would like to present to your souls, in conclusion here today. When we understand them and fill our souls with them; when we sense them and feel them, our hands are filled with the active compassion we will so often need. The contents of these seven lines are addressed to the other person, the sufferer, the one filled with pain; but in fact we say them to ourselves:

Rudolf Steiner: Notebook entry for the first aid course
(*Beiträge zur Rudolf Steiner Gesamtausgabe*, No. 108, 1992, p. 41)

Manuscript page by Rudolf Steiner (1914)
(*Beiträge zur Rudolf Steiner Gesamtausgabe*, No. 108, 1992, p. 46)

As long as you feel pain
That I avoid,
Christ remains unrecognized
At work in cosmic being;
For weak is the spirit
That can feel suffering
Only in its own body.[31]

*

World War I would continue for four years, transforming Europe into the "laboratory for a gigantic cemetery." (Tomáš Masaryk)

*

It was only after the war, with its catastrophic destruction and dissolution of old systems, that people in the anthroposophic movement came together with the presence of mind, courage, and awakened social conscience needed to take the initiative to implement Rudolf Steiner's basic suggestions in various fields of activity. The Stuttgart Waldorf School, anthroposophic medicine, curative education, biodynamic agriculture, and many social impulses began to take shape in the immediate post-war period as building blocks of a real "culture of selflessness" in the midst of destruction and chaos. Underlying all of these spiritual-scientifically based efforts was a readiness to delve into (and act out of) the existential situation of one's counterparts.[32] Implementing this process of will and cognition is "insightful selflessness" (218, 33). As Christ-imbued fields of human activity, anthroposophic medicine and curative education (along with Waldorf education and biodynamic agriculture) depend on the possibility of being completely open to the existential situation and needs of the Other, and on taking them as the basis for constructive intervention in world circumstances. Rudolf Steiner explicitly described and practiced selflessness as "the basic element in medicine" (315, 102).[33] In education grounded in spiritual science, it was the "gaze that is deepened in love."[34] Caroline von Heydebrand later had this to say about the unique character of Rudolf Steiner's work in the Stuttgart Waldorf School:

> It is characteristic of the Waldorf School that countless children there received remedies from Dr. Steiner — remedies that took each child's innermost nature into account.[35]

Not only Rudolf Steiner himself, however, but also all members of the General Anthroposophical Society belonged to a new Christian mystery community, and in this sense were meant to work selflessly as "forces for healing" in the world; that is, in the context of their very needy cultural environment. The Christmas Conference of 1923/24, one year after the destruction of the first Goetheanum, had ended with a corresponding call to carry the future-oriented therapeutic activity of the logos out into the world. In Rudolf Steiner's words:

> So, my dear friends, carry forth from here the warm hearts in which you have laid the foundation for the Anthroposophical Society. Go forth with these warm hearts to perform strong, health-bringing actions in the world. As a help to you, let your heads illuminate and purposefully guide your new intentions. This is what we resolve today to undertake with all our strength. (260, 284)

At that time, Rudolf Steiner gave a mantra to the nurses at the Arlesheim clinic. Through all the years that followed, Ita Wegman also focused intensively on this mantra, which was intimately connected to the Foundation Stone meditation and Christ's therapeutic activity:

> In the heart dwells,
> in radiant light,
> the human sense for helpfulness.
> In the heart works,
> in warming strength,
> the human power of love.
> So let us carry
> the soul's full will
> in heart's warmth
> and heart's light,
> that we may bring
> healing to those in need
> out of God's mercy.

(268, 310)[36]

*

Im Herzen wohnt
In leuchtender Helle
Des Menschen Helfersinn
Im Herzen wirket
In wärmender Macht
Des Menschen Liebekraft

So lasset uns tragen
Der Seele vollen Willen
In Herzens-Wärme
Und Herzens-Licht,
So wirken wir
Das Heil den Heilbedürft'gen
Aus Gottes Gnadensinn.

Handwritten mantra by Rudolf Steiner, 1923/24
(Ita Wegman Archive, Arlesheim)

In January of 1910, Rudolf Steiner began describing the future coming of Christ in the etheric, and indicated that the first breakthroughs in perceiving and connecting with the Christ would become possible in the 1930s: "Christ will stand beside human beings and become their counselor" (152, 91). Steiner also described that decade as a time of serious conflicts about the intended future of humanity; "the years 1933, 1934, and 1937 will be especially important" (118, 25).

On September 20, 1924, shortly before his final illness, Rudolf Steiner again spoke about the year 1933, this time in descriptions of the Apocalypse to priests of the Christian Community:

> Before human beings can grasp the etheric Christ in the right way, humanity will first have to finish dealing with the beast that emerges in 1933. I mean this in the apocalyptic sense. (346, 239ff.).

"Hatred of the spirit," said Rudolf Steiner as early as 1930, will emerge strongly from "both nationalism, on the one hand, and false socialism, on the other" (198, 82) as an unprecedented onslaught of evil.

And in fact, the year 1933 (eight years after Steiner's death) would see the beginning of the National Socialist reign of violence in Germany and Europe. Its demonic forces culminated in death and destruction of a scope previously unknown in the history of humanity: It triggered World War II and took 55 million lives; and with almost six million deaths, nearly exterminated the Jewish people, who once had been chosen to produce the bodily vehicle for the Christ Event. In a complete reversal and dramatic distortion of its healing mission,[37] the medical profession aided and abetted Adolf Hitler's "Reich of lower demons" (as Ernst Niekisch calls it)[38] in its effort to register and destroy all "unworthy" life. The Third Reich orchestrated abusive experimentation on, and ultimately the killing of, 260,000 ill and disabled people in a logical extension of the thinking first developed by nineteenth-century social Darwinist materialism.

> If current ways of teaching at our universities and current ways of thinking about social issues are simply allowed to continue for three more decades, Europe will have been laid to waste at the end of those thirty years. (Rudolf Steiner, 1919; 194, 197)

*

Rudolf Steiner described Ita Wegman as "standing under Michael."[39] In 1924, he had appointed her as head of the Medical Section at the Goetheanum.[40] In 1933, it was she who carried the spiritual and social responsibility for advancing the central healing mission of the anthroposophic movement. More than anyone else, she was prepared for the conflicts to come: "My work will always be to do battle with the demons."[41] At that time, she was preserving the substance and earthly reality of anthroposophic medicine and curative education; support- ing individual facilities and working groups; organizing effective protection for the patients and children entrusted to her care (as well as for her internationally active co-workers); and organiz- ing escape and rescue efforts, in large part for Jewish friends and acquaintances.[42] Her extreme activity was both warrior-like and selfless.[43] "The world situation looks so bad, it is as if everything must be done at a feverish pace before the great catastrophe sets in."[44] This activity was shared, however, by her many comrades- in-arms, whom she constantly encouraged and challenged "to work with the right attitude and actions so we can prevent some [of the evil]."[45] Reporting to an anthroposophic physician in London on her internationally directed activities, she wrote:

> To the extent possible, I am now attempting to organize expatriate Germans into a coalition to protest against the

anti-spirit now raging in Germany, and to prepare for times when it is once again possible to do something in Germany.[46]

Her uncompromising commitment to combat the demonic possession of fascism and evil in 1933 was followed by the crushing conflicts in Dornach. In the spring of 1934, Wegman fell seriously ill at age fifty-eight and was prepared to die; but experiencing the powerful support of Rudolf Steiner and the etheric Christ Being allowed her to overcome the illness and turn her destiny around. After an important trip to Palestine, she continued her work for nine additional years, well into World War II. "The spiritual world was not expecting me. In a meeting I had with Rudolf Steiner, at which the Christ Being was also present, I was challenged to continue to do something on earth. From that moment on, I gained the strength to take my recovery in hand."[47] In the end, Wegman also carried her healing, transcendent greatness of soul into the internal struggles in Dornach regarding the future of the General Anthroposophical Society— struggles characterized by the incursion of destructive forces into the arena of constructive progress Rudolf Steiner had left behind. Her death in the spring of 1943 had been preceded by acts of selfless forgiveness.[48] In Scotland, Karl König wrote about her in his diary:

> The child Kaspar [Hauser], the Buddha-like and mercurial bringer of peace, was ridiculed and ultimately killed by the adversarial forces. Like him, she was patient and quiet, because she carried the new Mercury staff, the sign of healing peace.[49]

In a letter dated April 10, 1935, five months after her return from Jerusalem, Ita Wegman wrote, in response to the question of why she did not defend herself more actively during the conflicts in Dornach:

> Spiritual beings need nourishment, spiritual nourishment that only human souls can provide. This nourishment comes from a specific soul-attitude of *voluntary self-sacrifice*. When souls can affirm and accept the severe tests that come toward them, good effects for the future can emerge.[50]

In the 1930s, Karl König also took the path opened and pointed out by Rudolf Steiner. Ultimately, this persecuted Jewish refugee and emigrant prevailed against all the forces of destruction that threatened his existence. Clearly with the help of higher powers, he succeeded in founding an internationally active Christian community for children with special needs; a community that began its work under the sign of selfless overcoming and self-sacrifice, and in the spirit of the Fifth Gospel.[51] Already as a child, König was constantly encountering Christianity. Each morning on his way to school, he was deeply moved by the words of Christ inscribed over the entrance to a hospital: "What you have done unto one of the least of my brothers, you have done unto me" (Matthew 25:40). He hid an image of Christ in his closet, and as a compassionate young adolescent during World War I, appalled by the destinies he encountered in the world, he selflessly gave away his clothing.[52] At sixteen, he wrote in his diary, "The world's suffering is in me."[53]

He decided to study medicine. "The sea of materialism is breaking over me, but I will stand fast."[54] That decision, and the path of social and medical intentions and good-heartedness that later led him to found the Camphill Movement, stood under this same sign. Both were shaped as much by retracing the suffering of Golgotha as by the light and warmth of the impending Christ Event. Early in life, König had cultivated forces of awe and wonder through his explorations of the marvel-filled world of embryology and the development of the human form. Forces of compassion and conscience were also fully active in him in the most exemplary way.[55] Clearly, they funneled active Christ impulses into König's activities. It was Ita Wegman who led him to the Sonnenhof in Arlesheim, and thus to anthroposophic curative education. Ten years later, she was one of the people who saved his life by facilitating his emigration to Scotland. The underlying principle of Camphill's esoteric Christian work was diametrically opposed to the "authorization to destroy life unworthy of living" and began confronting that practice in 1939. Through "observation immersed in love" as lived and taught by Rudolf Steiner, this work became an exemplary reality.[56] König wrote:

> For us, as students of Rudolf Steiner, the child (whatever his or her intellectual abilities may be) is more than what physical appearances reveal; more than the body, more than emotions, more than words spoken or unspoken, more even than accomplishments. The appearance is only the outer garment of an infinite and internal spiritual being. What does this mean? We are convinced of the unique existence of each human being, not only here on earth, but also as a spiritual being that exists before birth, and will continue to live after passing through the portal of death. Thus any intellectual or physical handicap is not the product of coincidence or misfortune. Its significance is specific to the individuality whose life it is attempting to change. Just as other people struggle against various illnesses, so too handicapped children must learn to overcome or live with their conditions. Our job as parents and teachers is to address the child's eternal being, so it may recognize its destiny. No matter how much the individuality may be obscured by layers of disability, paralysis, or uncontrolled emotions, we must attempt to breach these layers and get through to the holiest of holies in each human being: the place where the individual exists as spirit.
>
> The conviction that each human being is the carrier of an "I" that is eternal, immortal, and spiritual in origin is fundamental to our approach to the child. The child is our

brother, our sister, our equal, and the equal of all other human beings. We are not dealing with "handicapped children" but with children who have handicaps. Many of them are indeed mentally retarded, crippled, epileptic, mentally ill, lazy, or otherwise abnormal. Nonetheless, the inner core of their existence is not only infinite but holy and divine. They are all part of the godhead from which they came, to which they will return, and from which they will come again. This crippled and disfigured life is only one of many lives on their way back to the Father. We are all prodigal sons searching for the way back to the house of the eternal ground of the world, to the origin of our existence. This is the first essential characteristic of Camphill.[57]

*

As demonstrated by these accounts of the exemplary work and lives of Ita Wegman and Karl König, clearly the spiritual future-oriented processes of the 1930s, which happened parallel to and in dramatic conflict with the fateful events of that decade, were implemented primarily by individuals whose biographies were characterized both by existential perils *and* by the development of a soul-spiritual attitude of selfless readiness to make sacrifices, which became the standard for all their actions.[58] Although they endured times of almost unimaginable darkness, adversity, and menacing threats, these individuals also repeatedly experienced the unwavering support of a star that lead the way, a star they increasingly experienced and acknowledged as the "Sun of Christ." ("The good and purposeful intentions of all of you will come to your aid and illumine your minds. We must make this resolution today with all our strength. We shall find that if we prove worthy, a good star will shine on our intentions. My dear friends, follow that good star. By its light, we shall see where the gods want to lead us." Rudolf Steiner; 260, 284).

In his lecture in Basel on October 1, 1911, Rudolf Steiner had spoken about Christ's impending activity and how it would be experienced in the twentieth century:

> As they sit in their rooms alone, silent and oppressed with suffering and seeing no way forward, many will experience the door opening: The etheric Christ will appear and speak words of comfort to them. A living bearer of comfort—that is what the Christ will become for human beings. As strange as it may still sound today, it is nonetheless true that when people who see no way forward are sitting together waiting, even in a large group, they will see the etheric Christ. He will be there among them and will contribute his words to their gatherings. (130, 94)

During the National Socialist inferno, among the individuals who sat alone in their rooms or came together for advice, ultimately acting out of the purest forces, was Hans Scholl, a medical student from Munich. He was born on September 22, 1918, shortly before the end of World War I. Together with a few comrades (including his sister Sophie, who was three years younger) he mounted a decisive, publicly effective, and spiritually successful resistance to Adolf Hitler and the powers associated with him. The existing letters of Hans Scholl allow us to trace the inner path he followed in the founding and practices of the "White Rose"—a developmental journey that involved not only incisive experiences of battles and military hospitals, an intensive study of medical science, and an alert and ever-evolving faculty of judgment and conscience, but also an existential struggle with the Christ Event and theology, dominated by St. Augustine and the Dominican philosophy of Thomas Aquinas. The bookseller Josef Söhngen, a friend and associate of Hans Scholl, described Scholl's religious involvement, saying, "I have never met a young person who struggled with these things with such intensity and steadfastness."[59]

According to Rudolf Steiner, Jesus of Nazareth was beset by questions that lived powerfully in him during his preparation for the Christ Event of baptism in the Jordan—questions that arose out of the human situation and suffering of the time. As described above, Rudolf Steiner described Jesus' completion of this journey as the prerequisite to Paul's experience of the Christ and the encounter with the Christ Being in the etheric. Steiner's accounts from the Fifth Gospel were intended to prepare people for the tasks to come: "The souls that receive them now will certainly need them for the soul-spiritual work they will have to accomplish in the further course of humanity's evolution" (148, 324). On December 22, 1941, Hans Scholl looked back on his own inner journey in a letter to Carl Muth: "I heard the name of the Lord, and I heard Him speak. I sense a secure backing and I am confident in the goal I see."[60]

In the following year, Hans Scholl finally took action, distributing the first flyers of the White Rose, after receiving excerpts from the sermons of Clemens August von Galen, the Bishop of Münster, who had denounced from the pulpit the anti-Christian spirit of the National Socialist leadership (Hitler's "fathomless hatred of Christianity") and the already implemented "authorization to destroy life unworthy of living." He had said in part:

> For several months we have been hearing reports that Berlin has been arranging the forced abduction of long-term, seemingly incurable mental patients from treatment and nursing facilities. After a short time, their relatives receive routine notification that the patient has died and the body has been cremated; they are welcome to come pick up the ashes. The universal suspicion, bordering on certainty, prevails that so many unexpected deaths of mental patients cannot have occurred spontaneously, but must have been induced deliberately in accordance with the doctrine that it is permissible to destroy "life unworthy of living." That

is, to kill innocent people because they are thought to have no further value for the state and its populace. This is a terrible doctrine that seeks to justify the murder of innocents, and authorizes in principle the violent killing of invalids, cripples, the chronically ill, the senile, and the infirm.[61]

Subsequent White Rose flyers, compiled and distributed by Hans Scholl together with a few friends, expressly characterized Adolf Hitler's government as a "dictatorship of evil." The fourth flyer reads:

> Every word that comes out of Hitler's mouth is a lie. When he says peace, he means war; and when he invokes the name of the Almighty in the most outrageous manner, he means the force of evil, the fallen angel, Satan. His mouth is the gaping, stinking mouth of Hell, and his power is fundamentally depraved. Although we must indeed apply rational means in battling the terrorist National Socialist state, any modern person who still doubts in the literal existence of demonic forces has failed to comprehend the metaphysical background of this war. Behind the clear, sense-perceptible aspect, behind all rational, logical considerations lies the irrational; that is, the battle against the demons, the messengers of the Antichrist.
>
> We *must* attack evil where it is most powerful; namely, in the power of Hitler.[62]

Hans Scholl and his friends of the White Rose aspired to a "rebirth of the German spirit" and experienced the Christ event in the dimension of conscience.[63] For them, the moral obligations of conscience extended to current political events: "We will not be silent, for we are your bad conscience. The White Rose will not leave you in peace!"[64]

In late July 1941, Hans Scholl and the other students of his company were finally sent to Russia for three and a half months.

While there, he served again as a medic, and experienced the campaign of destruction mounted by the SS and portions of the Wehrmacht in occupied areas; but he also experienced the character of the eastern landscape and the Russian folk-spirit in very positive ways.[65] After receiving reports of his father's four-month incarceration for criticizing the regime, and after having now resolved to face all inner paths of sacrifice and transformation in the spirit of *imitatio Christi*, he wrote to his mother:

> I know only too well that very difficult times lie ahead for Father, alone in a narrow, gray space without any connection to the outside world. But he will endure. Because he is strong, he will be even stronger when he leaves prison for freedom again. I believe in the immeasurable power of suffering. True suffering is like a bath from which we emerge reborn. All that is great must first be purified before it is allowed to leave a human breast and be released into the wider world.[66]

To unite / the individual "I" / with the Cosmic "I." (260, 61)

*

On February 18, 1943, Hans Scholl and his sister Sophie were spotted tossing flyers that called for the establishment of a "new spiritual Europe" from the atrium of the University in Munich, and were promptly arrested.[67] On February 22, 1943 (the last birthday of Ita Wegman, who died a short time later), the two siblings and their friend Christoph Probst were beheaded. The execution came three days before Hans Scholl was to have met with Dietrich Bonhoeffer in Berlin; and it came after five days of imprisonment, which they spent in a state of calm and equanimity that was incomprehensible to both their fellow prisoners and their guards.

Everyone who still had contact with them in those days—fellow prisoners, prison chaplains, guards, even Gestapo officials—were extremely impressed with their bravery and their dignified behavior.[68] ...They were so phenomenally brave. Everyone in the prison was impressed. That's why we risked getting the three of them together for a moment before the execution. (If word had gotten out, there would have been severe consequences for us.) We wanted them to be able to smoke a last cigarette together. It was just a few minutes, but I think it meant a lot to them. "I didn't know dying could be so easy," said Christoph Probst, and then he added, "In a few minutes we will see each other again in eternity." Then they were led off, the girl first, unblinking. We didn't understand how it was possible.[69] The executioner said he had never seen anyone die like that.[70]

After the war, Hans Scholl had wanted to work not only as a physician, but also on behalf of a fundamental renewal of the social order in the spirit of freedom. Just a few hours before his death, he said to his parents in a Christological, Michaelic turn of phrase, "There is no hatred in me. Everything is behind me now."[71] Looking back on the end of her siblings' lives, Inge Scholl wrote: "For them at that time, Christ became a unique big brother who was always there with them, even closer than death."[72]

*

In their brief earthly lives, Hans Scholl and his friends had "battled in full consciousness against the evil that appears in humanity's evolution" (Steiner, 1917; 178, 175). At the end of life, they had grown far beyond themselves, their actions based on a spiritual stance and certitude that were at least connected with, if not identical to, the living forces of the Christ. Four weeks after Hans Scholl's birth, on October 25, 1918,

Rudolf Steiner had said in Dornach that "the experience of evil" in the near future would "make it possible for the Christ to reappear" and "stand beside" human beings (185,104).[73] In Kristiania [Oslo] five years earlier, Rudolf Steiner had begun his lectures on the Fifth Gospel, which were probably intended not only for earthly audiences, but were also significant for the spiritual world, and thus perhaps also for human souls about to set forth on their earthly path: "The souls who take this up now will most certainly need it for the soul-spiritual work they must accomplish in the further course of humanity's evolution" (148, 324).

*

Dresden, February 2, 1945

3

The Connection to Rudolf Steiner

Selflessness is essential to true anthroposophy.

—RUDOLF STEINER (GA 220, 152)

Rudolf Steiner (1861-1925)

RUDOLF STEINER'S own journey through life, which made anthroposophy possible on earth, also took place under the sign of definitive selflessness. Marie Steiner, who accompanied his steps and his work most closely for more than two decades, called his a *"life of voluntary sacrifice."*[74]

Rudolf Steiner's path was characterized by the greatest possible inner activity and by absolute, consciously directed engagement of will. These led him to reject, vehemently and at an early age, any "pseudo-ethical" orientation and passive methods of "selfless" (but actually egocentric) esthetic altruism.[75] He always focused on the importance of the independent human "I" to all means of cognition and action. In his first major publication at age twenty-five, on Goethe, Steiner already emphasized that Goethe's forward-looking scientific research (and approach to the world) were characterized by "borrowing" his mode of observation from the specific aspects of the outer world that he was observing, rather than imposing his own mode of observation upon them (2, 21). At the end of the eighteenth century, Goethe had said that people in search of knowledge needed to "subdue self-centeredness" and "increase objectivity" in order to derive "standards of knowledge and data for coming to conclusions, not from themselves, but from the circle of things they observe."[76] In other words, "inwardly identifying" with the object under observation is what makes it possible to develop theories and acquire insight. In this way, for Goethe (and for Steiner) the natural environment becomes the "teacher of selflessness" (12, 35) in the pursuit of a method of research that aspires to develop specific organs of perception for cosmic connections, and that is infused both with devotion *and* with the ultimate in energetic will. Rudolf Steiner contributed fundamentally to the development of this Goethean approach to cognition, making it the basis of a Christian Rosicrucian path of training that then led to anthroposophic spiritual science, and thus to a scientific means of researching the spiritual world in "complete inner selflessness" (9, 138). After a certain developmental stage in Rudolf Steiner's biography, this *"insightful selflessness"* (218, 22) was carried out in inner union with the forces and intentions of the living Christ.[77] Friedrich Rittelmeyer offers the following description of Rudolf Steiner's exemplary, subtly differentiated ability to spiritually perceive the other person in "insightful selflessness":

> I have never seen another human being observe as attentively as he could; not moving at all, but in selfless devotion. It was as if he were recreating the other person anew in some subtle aspect of his own soul that he made available for that purpose. He was not "thinking" about the other person; it was more of an inner, spiritual act of recreating that person, which revealed the entire course of the person's becoming.[78]

*

In a seminal comment in one of his lectures on the Fifth Gospel (Cologne, December 18, 1913), Rudolf Steiner made it clear that his research into the concrete events of the beginning of the Christian era in the akashic record required complete relinquishing of self on the researcher's part. Past events (or rather, soul-spiritual processes undergone in the course of these events) are preserved in the substance of the cosmic memory of exalted spiritual beings: "The true realities of the cosmos are beings in various states of consciousness" (148, 306). For human cognition to be able to penetrate such realities, however, total submission to these beings is required; or rather, a process of real self-sacrifice. Steiner expected or hoped that those who had heard him speak would retrace the human path of suffering of Jesus of Nazareth in a way that was both receptively empathetic and actively willed. He himself had already undergone and suffered an extreme form of this process in an inward-looking, cognitive path of sacrifice, which he was able to endure and master only with the help of Christian forces of resurrection:

> Anything related to the soul's penetration of an individual event can be researched only when the soul makes sense of these words: The soul offers itself up as food to the primal beginnings, or Archai; to the Spirits of Personality. Strange as this statement may sound, it is nonetheless true that concrete realities such as the life of Jesus of Nazareth cannot be researched unless we understand that we are "eaten" by, and serve as nourishment for, the Spirits of Personality. ... Human beings are to the Archai as grains of wheat are to you as a physical human being. We must not only know this on a theoretical level, but also relate to the Archai with the consciousness of a grain of wheat being ground to mush between human teeth, and then passing the palate and entering the stomach. Just as that grain of wheat might know, "I am food for this human being," so too we must know, "I am food for the Archai; I am being digested by the Archai; I am living their life in them." Acknowledging this living reality means being transported into the consciousness of the Archai, the Spirits of Personality.... The circumstances of our experience must change if we intend to enter higher worlds and read their contents. If we want to research concrete facts in humanity's evolution, facts such as the life of Jesus of Nazareth, we must know that we are being digested by the Spirits of Personality.

Perhaps these remarks will serve to illustrate how totally different esoteric research is from research in the outer world. It is quite possible to think this image through, and it provides you with important clues. Imagine yourself in the place of a grain of wheat as it is ground to mush between the teeth. This is an accurate analogy of reading the consciousness of the Archai. We must feel that our souls are being crushed. In other words, higher research is not possible without inner tragedy and suffering. Unlike research in the physical world, any higher research that attempts to be more than just a fantasy cannot be so abstract that it does not cause pain (148, 309 ff).

In this sense, the "higher research" on which Rudolf Steiner based the messages he conveyed from the Fifth Gospel was conducted in radical selflessness and left its imprint on the style of delivery of his subsequent lectures:

> Steiner's words were filled with love for the helpless baby when he spoke about Jesus, and with the glow of the virgin's suffering when he spoke about the Christ; suffering born of love intersected with love born of suffering. No one else could do what Rudolf Steiner did when he presented his Christology to human souls. This was not cognition in the conventional sense; it was all forms of overflowing love and overflowing suffering.
>
> On such occasions, the sign his face bore was an expression of his state of consciousness, and roused his listeners from sleep: *ICH*. [In German, *Ich* means "I"; but the writer, Andrei Belyi, is also using it as an acronym for *"Iesus Christos"*] Before he began to speak about the Christ, he stood in front of us in austere silence. (Andrei Belyi)[79]

At the same time, however, Rudolf Steiner's research on Christ Jesus was also a very intimate process of receiving and bestowing blessing, and thus of highest revelation; a response that fulfilled and imbued his Christian esoteric path of selflessness:

> I will never forget seeing him as a wise man who had become a shepherd, simple and filled with love, devoted to the child. I see his pale face above the lectern, pale with

a strange white sheen that reflected no color at all. I had never even suspected that such white, pure light could exist. A purple glow emanated from his Christ-imbued words, and the words of Revelation 2:17 came to mind: "To the one who overcomes, I will give a white stone with a new name written on it, a name known only to the one who receives it." (Andrei Belyi)[80]

*

In this sense, Rudolf Steiner's own biography and path of knowledge were the vehicle and expression of "insightful self-lessness" in approaching spiritual/physical world realities. The path taken by this "leading Christian initiate and present-day follower of Christ" (Prokofieff) was essential to the creation of a future social culture worthy of humanity under the auspices of the coming Christ. From the beginning, however, the reception of anthroposophy and all efforts to establish it on earth depended on the success of his audiences and his coworkers in following the same path. Rudolf Steiner repeatedly described the selflessness individuals needed to develop as an integral component of the path of esoteric schooling, and as an essential element in both anthroposophic research *and* the reception of anthroposophy. ("Selflessness is essential to true anthroposophy." 220, 152). In 1921, he explained in greater detail in a lecture to theologians:

> You see, with regard to what individuals gain for themselves in anthroposophy, no matter what the extent of their own research or insight ..., they must give up a great deal of the "I"; that is, their egotism. In a certain sense, a degree of selflessness is required in order to leave oneself behind and merge into the world. Many aspects of habitual egotism must be radically expunged in order to develop a truly human relationship to even the simplest anthroposophic

insights. A strong sense of the world must be developed to counteract the sense of self. Then, while following what appears to be a path of knowledge, the most ardent love begins to grow. Basically, we really can learn to surrender to objectivity in the pursuit of anthroposophical content. (343, 97)

Steiner tells us that selflessness *and* self-confidence—that is, the foundation of the higher "I"—are essential prerequisites to treading the path of anthroposophy:

For example, I have experienced the following phenomenon: Good anthroposophists strive with might and main to find their way to anthroposophy, but *without the necessary degree of either selflessness or self-confidence*. They then lose courage, and instead join a Catholic religious order. This is not a hypothetical example; I am telling you what I have experienced. These people resisted being so intensely present. They then lost courage and looked for something to hold on to, something that would provide a certain inner satisfaction, which is actually only some kind of internalized lust or pleasure, while they surrendered to the activity. So they joined Catholic orders. (343, 108; italics added)

Repeatedly and extremely clearly, Rudolf Steiner emphasized the need for receptivity to his messages about Jesus and the Christ, drawn from the Fifth Gospel. He was hoping his audiences would prove capable of following the contents he presented with existential selflessness *and* with full I-consciousness. (*"Is there no one here who has a question for me?"*)[81] He had undertaken to reveal these contents only at a very specific time; clearly, his intentions were to prepare and school his audiences. As Andrei Belyi reported, the necessary receptivity was present only in Oslo (Norway), not in the anthroposophic branches in

Germany, where Rudolf Steiner gave only a brief recapitulation of the material before falling silent on the subject of the Fifth Gospel. Belyi tells us, "The same 'sleepiness' spread to every center. The thorns were already piercing him; the contents he hoped to disclose were shrouded. It became obvious to Steiner that the Fifth Gospel was not being received appropriately."[82] After mentioning the Fifth Gospel in the first few months of 1914, the year the war began, Steiner never returned to the subject again.[83]

*

Not continuing (or, from the spiritual-social perspective, not being able to continue) his messages about the life of Christ Jesus did not end Rudolf Steiner's self-sacrificing efforts to pave the way for a future culture of Pauline-oriented selflessness. He continued this work in many different fields of activity, stepping up his efforts in the final fifteen months of his life, after the ritual laying of the Foundation Stone for the General Anthroposophical Society, with its decidedly Christological impulse for the future. Rudolf Steiner implicitly assured the human community he had fostered that he would continue to support its tasks on behalf of civilization from the spiritual world after the end of his earthly life; this was suggested by many of his own comments and his overall concept of the section-based administration of the School for Spiritual Science *through him*.[84] Moreover, this assurance had its deep and lasting esoteric foundation in the Johannine spirit of all his activity as a Christian initiate in association or even in "intimate communion" with Christ (26, 92). (*"I tell you, whoever takes my "I" into himself will also be able to do what I am doing; and he will do greater things still because I am going to the Father. Anything you ask in my name, I will do so, that the Father may be glorified in the Son's work. Everything you ask in my name I will do. ... He who knows my cosmic goals and takes them into his will, he it is who truly loves me."* John 14:12-14, 21).

In der Zeiten Wende
Trat das Welten- Geistes - Licht
In den irdischen Wesensstrom;
Nacht- Dunkel
Hatte ausgewaltet;
Taghelles Licht
Erstrahlte in Menschenseelen;
Licht,
Das erwärmet
Die armen Hirtenherzen;
Licht,
Das erleuchtet
Die weisen Königshäupter.

Göttliches Licht,
Christus - Sonne
Erwärme
Unsere Herzen;
Erleuchte
Unsere Häupter;

Dass gut werde,
Was wir
Aus Herzen gründen;
Was wir
Aus Häuptern führen,
Wollen.

Rudolf Steiner, 1923/24 (GA 260, addendum, pp. 44-45)

At the turning point of time
The Spirit-Light of the world
Entered the stream of earthly being.
Darkness of night
Had held its sway,
Day-radiant light
Streamed into the souls of human beings;
Light that gives warmth
To simple shepherds' hearts;
Light that enlightens
The wise heads of kings.

Light Divine,
Christ-Sun,
Warm our hearts,
Enlighten our heads,
That good may become
What we would found from our hearts,
What we would direct from our heads,
In conscious
Willing.

For his successors, their binding relationship to Rudolf Steiner in his eternal individuality, and as the earthly representative and bearer of the active Christ Being, became the incisive basis for their further work. As Steiner had suggested in an early lecture in Zurich on December 3, 1916:

> A tremendous amount would be gained if that *selflessness* were extended to such an extent that those living later would join forces with the dead, and make a conscious attempt to truly maintain continuity in evolution. Whether the relationship is purely one of choice or brought about by karma, *our connection to those attempting to allow their activity to radiate from the spiritual world is something of tremendous importance; that is, if the connection is consciously experienced and acted upon.* (168, 214; italics added)

Rudolf Steiner's closest colleagues, such as Marie Steiner and Ita Wegman, saw clearly that anthroposophy would continue to develop as a positive force in civilization only through connections to Rudolf Steiner that are imbued with selflessness, not distorted by "post-modern" desires for autonomy. They also realized that the future culture of selflessness that was being created required a selfless connection to the individual who had prepared the way for the coming Christ at the dawn of the Michaelic age. If, as Rudolf Steiner put it, *"only through achieving selflessness will it be possible to hold humanity back from the brink of destruction"* (93, 123), then the spiritual work of anthroposophy in connection with Rudolf Steiner, and on behalf of the general fate of humanity and the earth, must be maintained at all costs; it must be incorporated into and transform the future:

> There is one thing we must realize clearly: that what was once provided as spiritual substance must be transformed into a sacrificial vessel before new revelations can occur. When groups of people succeed in taking in and working

with Rudolf Steiner's spiritual legacy in a way that allows this vessel to take shape, then the moment has come when help will arrive from spiritual worlds. It may come soon or it may still take a long time; that is under our control. (Ita Wegman; March 30, 1941)[85]

*

Victorious spirit,
May your flames
Fill the weakness
Of faint-hearted souls.
Burn out all egotism;
Let selflessness,
Humanity's life-stream,
Well up as the source
Of spiritual rebirth. (268, 73)

*

Rudolf Steiner tells us that Michael, as the spirit of our age, is now fighting in the spiritual sphere closest to the earth on behalf of the approach of the Christ Being (156, 56). This struggle also radiates into the human being—specifically, into the human heart: *"Within the human being an etheric image of Michael is active, engaged in a struggle that will gradually allow the human being to become free; for it is not Michael who is waging this battle, but human devotion and the image of Michael that it evokes"* (223, 102). Rudolf Steiner laid the Foundation Stone of the General Anthroposophical Society in the depths of the etheric heart-organ, as a "stone of love" under the sign of the coming Christ, thinking back to the beginning of the Christian era in active preparation for the present and future revelation of "Divine Light" and the "Sun of Christ" in the etheric realm—the beginning of the culture of selflessness.[86]

Appendix

Ita Wegman

The Mystery of the Earth (1929)[87]

Ita Wegman (1942)

THE EARTH IS the setting for human evolution. This has not always been the case, however, since humanity's ultimate origins lie in spirit and soul, for which the human body is only a vessel. The evolution of this vessel is the history both of the human race on earth, and of our earthly surroundings. If our evolution had been limited to the physical vessel, we would be looking at the evolution of an animal. The vessel is made human by the human spirit and soul. But what connects spirit and soul to the bodily human element? Because no earthly substance would have been able to effect this connection, a heavenly substance had to insert itself into the earth so the soul-spirit could dwell in the body.

The substances we find on earth have been excreted by life processes in the earthly environment. We see this quite clearly in the case of calcium, which was excreted by the animal life of primeval seas. Most substances we now habitually think of as inorganic reveal themselves to spiritual research as having emerged from life processes in the earthly environment. In primeval times, this life was a unity that differentiated into individual organisms only during the second geological epoch.

Some substances, however, such as the metals, came about in a different way. They are the influences of planets that radiate into the earth from the cosmos. Iron occupies a unique position among the metals, because instead of simply radiating in, it was left behind as a substance in the gaseous state at a time when the Earth and Mars orbits intersected. The substance thus introduced into earthly evolution enables spirit and soul, the cosmic element in human beings, to connect to the earthly element. Just as a magnet attracts iron, iron attracts the element of spirit and soul. Iron is a significant component of the warm blood that houses the spirit and soul element, the human "I," on the bodily level. Thus we see iron as guiding the cosmic element down into the earthly element. The entire first half of the Earth epoch of evolution, therefore, stands under the sign of iron. But in the course of earthly existence, once human beings have awakened to the full power of the "I" pervading the bodily vessel from the inside out, they begin to turn back to the cosmos.

The meaning of the Earth epoch of evolution lies in this turning back to the cosmos, which human beings could not possibly accomplish through their own strength. Humanity would never have been able to bring about this complete reversal of the direction of earthly evolution. At the midpoint of the earth's and humanity's evolution, therefore, a cosmic impulse had to insert itself into the course of evolution. This happened through the descent to earth of a cosmic being, the exalted Sun Being himself, the Christ, who united himself with everything earthly through his death on the cross, thus transforming the earth in its inmost nature. The seed thus planted supplies the goal and direction for the events of all subsequent epochs. Until then, human beings had been controlled by the forces working in the stream of heredity and in the blood, but from that point onward the individual element became the deciding factor. Christ became the spirit of humanity as a whole; but at the same time, he also guides each individual so that humanity's common goal can emerge from the progress of developing individuals.

The human "I," the most individual aspect of each human being, has the unique quality of not wanting to remain self-contained. Instead, it wants to immerse itself in the being of the Other. What we know as lower selfishness or egotism is totally foreign to the "I." Since the Mystery of Golgotha, therefore, everything that truly connects people is based on individual impulses, and thus on freedom. In the process of understanding our fellow human beings and submitting to their individual thoughts, in the moments when we receive the contents of their consciousness, we extinguish the contents of our own consciousness. Truly listening to another person is an act of extreme selflessness. When two people come together in freedom, recognizing each other in spirit, the old traditional symbol of the

Mercury staff becomes a perceptible reality in spirit. A portion of each person's I-organization leaves the body, submerges in the other person, and then returns to its own body. These two inter-penetrating I-activities, which are associated with two souls, are the two snakes that twine upward around the staff of the spirit of truth. Thus Mercury leads human beings to freedom. In the new community, free individuals find each other in the spirit of truth, and the perception of truth becomes love. This is why Rudolf Steiner said in his book *The Threshold of the Spiritual World* that love is experiencing the Other in one's own soul.

This is how individuals meet through Christ. It is Christ who allows one human "I" to awaken to another, and individuals unrelated by blood to become brothers and sisters. The ancient Mysteries foresaw this transition from a community of blood relationships to a community of freedom, and called the two halves of earthly evolution Mars and Mercury, respectively.

Where these things were known, Mercury was recognized as the "dissolver" who released people from their old ties and led them to freedom and to new, consciously willed connections. Thus everything soluble was called "mercurial." In the human body, this dissolving element is realized in the circulation of flu-ids, which initiation science also associates with the forces of Mercury. A person's temperament depends on the character of the flow of fluid in the body. If the rhythm of these flows is in harmony with the rhythm of the blood, the person's tempera-ment is "sanguine," named after the blood, *sanguis.* If the flow of fluid lags behind the rhythm of the blood, its movement becomes viscous and mucilaginous, and the associated temperament is called "phlegmatic." Then again, if the flow of fluid is more rapid, as is normally the case with bile, the associated tempera-ment is called "choleric." "Melancholic" describes a tempera-ment characterized not by movement of enlivened fluids (fluid "circulation" almost no longer applies here), but by the sluggish-ness of the substances themselves, which causes fluids to back up or stagnate.

Our evolutionary goal as human beings is to balance all four temperaments harmoniously within ourselves, which happens when body, soul, and spirit are in balance. Each one of us is meant to develop a free soul that holds the balance between the sense-perceptable and spirituality. If the bodily element predominates, the person is melancholic. If the fire of the spirit prevails, the noble aspects of the choleric temperament are revealed. The soul element can appear in one of two nuances: The spirit endows it with sanguine mobility, the body endows it with phlegmatic sluggishness. All of these combinations (how the upper relates to the lower, the dominant to the dominated, the spiritual to the sensory) were once seen as expressions of Mercury, the being of many forms. People sensed that Mercury mediated the interpenetration of individual and divine existence and expressed this particular aspect of Mercury in the symbol of two interpenetrating triangles that form a harmonious six-pointed star. "Destiny" is the name we customarily give to the divine existence that pervades human beings. When we bring body, soul, and spirit into harmony, we make our peace with destiny; we have learned to accept and love it. Individuals who can do so are ready to face destiny's challenges.

In the Mysteries of antiquity, it was Mercury who guided human souls over the threshold into the spiritual world. In the Christian era, Mercury not only leads us to the wisdom of the suprasensory, but also guides our conscious connection to new threads of destiny, so we learn to release the old and allow the new that brings healing to arise out of acts of love. The human organization in all its members is shaped in accordance with destiny, woven out of the deeds of previous earthly lives. Bringing about healing requires conscious new deeds directed from one person to another. Thus Mercury can contribute insight and impulses to act. Mercury facilitates the awakening of one human "I" on another so that, thus awakened, it may work into the future through healing activity. Mercury, therefore, is the great teacher of reincarnation and karma, enabling individuals and groups of individuals to understand each other consciously so they can work toward their common goal.

Belief in reincarnation and karma is not new; in the East it was kept alive, but in the West it was forgotten for hundreds of years before it reappeared in Christianized form in the nineteenth century. Now the concepts of reincarnation and karma include not only repeated earthly lives and human destinies, but also the connections of individuals to each other and to the earth. The Christianizing of these teachings consists in recognizing that the earth's destiny is included in human destinies. Buddhist teachings still turned away from the earth, but Christian teachings must turn toward it. The human beings living on earth today must now feel increasingly responsible for the destiny of planet Earth itself.

Through our modern transportation and information systems, humanity has begun to encompass the earth as a whole. Outwardly, in fact, we have essentially taken full possession of it. The consequence for humanity is unprecedented: a destined connection to the earth as a whole. We must become increasingly conscious of this big picture.

In antiquity, human beings were required to assume only very limited responsibility, while guidance of the world was left to the gods. By the eighteenth century, humanity believed it necessary to assume responsibility at least for the social realm; while nature, although no longer seen as divine, was still held to be governed by laws independent of human beings. In recent times, however, technology has allowed us to control and dominate the forces of nature. As a result, we have become responsible for certain aspects of nature, and we shall soon see how this responsibility unfolds.

Formerly, with isolated exceptions, natural processes were clearly separated from historical events. Increasingly, they are now merging. The glorious Renaissance city of Venice stands in the sea on pilings cut from forests that once covered the mountains of Dalmatia. Deforestation of this area triggered climatic changes that have since intensified. This is one small example of the larger instances we can expect to see in the future.

This new relationship to nature also applies to the human constitution itself. Educators and physicians confront a bit of the natural world in each person's heredity; and increasingly, their task is to reshape it. If humanity neglects this task, we will soon confront natural phenomena that we ourselves have caused without realizing that we are doing so. We will find no explanations for the phenomena that emerge. Nature, formerly governed by eternal laws, will seem to devolve into chaos. We stand at the very beginning of this global situation. Nature is becoming a mirror of chaotic human behavior, as is evident in catastrophes and anomalies; we perceive them in nature's mirror without recognizing them as our own reflection.

The natural sciences seek to exclude the human subject from their concepts of the natural world. Until these concepts are adapted to include connections to human beings, they will be useless for understanding the transformations that are now occurring. Our image of nature must be expanded to include human beings. A philosophy that does so is called "anthroposophy" with good reason. Recognizing that nature in all its aspects has only been waiting for the human being, so to speak, is an insight that does not leave the human heart cold, but kindles enthusiasm for action. We must allow our actions to infuse all aspects of life with the results of the transformations we have each been able to effect through our moral struggles with those small portions of nature that are our bodies.

As a motif of nature, the human body is the result of the first half of the Earth epoch in evolution. In this respect, we are the crown of creation. Now we must transform ourselves and allow our deeds to flow into the earth as the result of what we have transformed in ourselves. The second half of Earth evolution lies dormant in human beings, and we must awaken it. Then the divine element that has abandoned cosmic form to become human will find the way back to the cosmos through human deeds. When these deeds are performed out of the right impulse, the mercurial element of healing is at work.

Thus the divine element has relinquished its exclusive claim to power and glory, and has shifted responsibility for the entire universe to human beings so we can become free. We humans can take initiative, but our actions would remain weak if we acted alone. But we can be certain that if we enliven our thinking, apply our freedom, and allow a new element to emerge within us, the divine world will stand by us and provide the powerful help needed to complete what we have initiated out of right insight and freedom.

The signs of the times speak to us in unambiguous language. The natural world is changing, and it poses serious questions to us: Do we want to transform our thinking? Do we choose to recognize that the cosmic challenge that appears to us in chaos and suffering need not mean destruction, but rather the spiritualization of humanity?

This, then, is where we stand in the course of human and earthly evolution. In reality, humanity's evolution *is* Earth evolution. This new thinking has already approached us; we must simply seize hold of it with courage, and implement it conscientiously in all areas of life. What we do now must pave the way for this new thinking.

Notes

References from the works of Rudolf Steiner given in the text
and the following notes refer to the pages of the German editions
(GA). All passages have been newly translated to give consistency
of terminology.

1   Works by Rudolf Steiner cited in the text and notes are listed
    as: (Gesamtausgabe volume number, page number). GA vol-
    umes cited are listed in the bibliography.
2   See Peter Selg: *Maria Krehbiel-Darmstädter. Von Gurs nach
    Auschwitz. Der innere Weg.* Arlesheim 2010.
3   Ibid., p. 122.
4   Andrei Belyi: *Verwandeln des Lebens.* Basel 1975, p. 469.
5   See, among others, Eric Hobsbawm: *The Age of Extremes:
    The Short Twentieth Century, 1914–1991.* New York 1994;
    and Mark Mazower: *Dark Continent: Europe's 20th Century.*
    New York 1998.
6   Assya Turgenieff: *Erinnerungen an Rudolf Steiner und die
    Arbeit am ersten Goetheanum.* Stuttgart 1972, p. 61.
7   Hilde Boos-Hamburger: *Aus Gesprächen mit Rudolf Steiner
    über Malerei und einige Erinnerungen an die Zeit des ersten
    Goetheanum.* Basel 1954, p. 7.
8   Natalie Turgenieff-Pozzo: *Zwölf Jahre der Arbeit am
    Goetheanum. 1913-1925.* Dornach 1942, p. 14ff.
9   On contemporary developments in research into the life
    of Jesus, see (among others) David Hoffman's overview:
    "Von Jesus zu Christus. Rudolf Steiner und die Leben-
    Jesu-Forschung seiner Zeit." In: *Beiträge zur Rudolf Steiner
    Gesamtausgabe 102,* Easter 1989, pp. 2-55, as well as Albert
    Schweitzer's comprehensive monograph: *Geschichte der
    Leben-Jesu Forschung.* 9th edition, Tübingen 1984. On events
    related to the Theosophical Society's efforts to promote the
    Hindu youth Jiddu Krishnamurti as the second physical
    incarnation of Christ, see (among others) Hella Wiesberger:

"Die Trennung von der 'Esoteric School of Theosophy' und der 'Theosophical Society'" in: *Rudolf Steiners esoterische Lehrtätigkeit*. Dornach 1997, pp. 133ff.

10   Belyi: loc. cit. p. 469.

11   See Peter Selg: *Rudolf Steiner und das Fünfte Evangelium*, pp. 57ff and 88ff. [In English: *Rudolf Steiner and the Fifth Gospel*. Tr. Catherine Creeger. SteinerBooks: Great Barrington, MA 2010].

12   On these "spatial" aspects, see Rudolf Steiner's detailed descriptions of December 30, 1913 (GA 149), which were not repeated in subsequent lectures.

13   On the related question of the human connection to Christ's resurrection body ("phantom") and on the possibility of the receiving of "images" of the Christ-I, see in particular Rudolf Steiner's fundamental explanations in his lectures *The Principle of Spiritual Economy* (GA 109), and in the Karlsruhe lecture cycle *From Jesus to Christ* (GA 131), as well as Sergei O. Prokoffieff's elaborations on this subject in his books *Rudolf Steiner und die Grundlegung der neuen Mysterien* (Stuttgart 1982) [In English: *Rudolf Steiner and the Founding of the New Mysteries*. Temple Lodge Publishing: London 1994]; *"Menschen mögen es hören." Das Mysterium der Weihnachtstagug* (Stuttgart 2002) [In English: *May Human Beings Hear It! The Mystery of the Christmas Conference*. Temple Lodge Publishing: Forest Row, U.K. 2004]; *Die Grundsteinmeditation. Ein Schlüssel zu den neuen christlichen Mysterien* (Dornach 2003) [In English: *The Foundation Stone Meditation. A Key to the Christian Mysteries*. Tr. Maria St. Goar. Temple Lodge Publishing: Forest Row, U.K. 2007]; and *Was ist Anthroposophie?* (Dornach 2004) [In English: *What is Anthroposophy?* Temple Lodge Publishing: Forest Row, U.K. 2006].

14   See note 15.

15   Toward the end of his lecture in Cologne on May 8, 1912, immediately after describing the three bodily sheaths of the present and future Christ Impulse or Christ Spirit, Rudolf Steiner spoke directly about the possibility and necessity of a

sculptural representation of the figure of Christ: "Why can we say these things now? Because the problem of how to depict the figure of Christ as it really is in various aspects of life is now being resolved. We will behold it as it is only by considering some of the findings of spiritual research. We cannot look back on what existed in Palestine, because then Christ was using the sheaths of Jesus" (143, 185). In Cologne Steiner made only brief mention of the forces of wonder, compassion, and conscience that shape the countenance of Christ. In a lecture in Berlin six days later (May 14, 1912), however, he spoke in greater detail, emphasizing the artistic aspect (133, 115ff.) In that lecture in Berlin, Rudolf Steiner also introduced the importance of the forces of wonder, compassion, and conscience that humanity must develop, speaking of them as the "purpose of the Earth phase of evolution (133, 106) and as the organs ("sheaths") that would allow the earth to become imbued with the Christ in successive stages: "When the earth reaches its goal, it (like the human being) will be a completely developed entity that corresponds to the Christ Impulse" (133, 113). See also Steiner's wording fourteen days later in Norrköping: "When the earth has achieved its goal and human beings have understood the right moral impulses that bring about everything that is good, then the Christ Impulse, which flowed into humanity's evolution like an "I" through the Mystery of Golgotha, will be released. It will be enclosed in an astral body made of faith, of all human deeds of wonder and awe, in something resembling an etheric body made of deeds of love, and in something resembling a physical body shaped by deeds of conscience" (155, 113ff.).

16   Rudolf Steiner, personal communication to Willem Zeylmans van Emmichoven, Dornach, December 18, 1920, as quoted in Willem Zeylmans van Emmichoven: "Rudolf Steiner in Holland." In: M. J. Krück von Poturzyn (ed.): *Wir erlebten Rudolf Steiner. Erinnerungen seiner Schüler.* 3rd edition, Stuttgart 1967, p. 253.

17   Willem Zeylmans van Emmichoven: *Der Grundstein.* 6th edition, Stuttgart 1990, p. 11. [In English: *The Foundation*

Stone. Tr. John Davy. Temple Lodge Publishing: Forest Row, U.K. 2002].

18   See note 13; and this statement by Sergei O. Prokofieff: "Christ is the only being in any world who can enter the human "I" without extinguishing it. To the contrary, Christ infinitely enhances individual forces and capacities, because the being of the cosmic "I" is identical to that of the human being." (Prokofieff: *"Menschen mögen es hören." Das Mysterium der Weihnachtstagnung,* p. 48). [In English: *May Human Beings Hear It! The Mystery of the Christmas Conference.* Tr. Maria St. Goar. Forest Row, U.K.: Temple Lodge 2004].

19   On the differences in sensory organization in animals, see (for example) Rudolf Steiner's explanations of March 1, 1919. After describing the reduced vascularization (and vitality) of the eye in humans in comparison to animals, he says that it is well known to the natural sciences that the eyes of lower animals include blood-filled structures that actively create a connection between the interior of the eye and the entire body. (Such as the *pecten oculi,* a comb-like structure of blood vessels belonging to the choroid in the eye of a bird. It is non-sensory and is a pigmented structure that projects into the vitreous body from the point where the optic nerve enters the eyeball. The pecten is believed to both nourish the retina and control the pH of the vitreous body. It is present in all birds and some reptiles. In the vertebrate eye, blood vessels lie in front of the retina, partially obscuring the image. The pecten helps to solve this problem, lifting the blood vessels away from the retina and leading to the extremely sharp eyesight of birds such as hawks. The pigmentation of the pecten is believed to protect the blood vessels against damage from ultraviolet light.) The human eye lacks these structures, but is much more independent. Sensory independence (the emancipation of the senses from the organization of the body as a whole) appears only in humans. As a result, the entire world of the senses has much more connection to the will in humans than in animals. ...

In animals, the senses are not flooded with will but with a deeper-lying element, so the animal sensory system is more intimately connected to the organism as a whole. Humans live much more strongly in the outer world; animals tend to live more in their own inner world" (188, pp. 24ff.). In this connection, Rudolf Steiner focused in various lectures on the "death experience" specific to the etherically reduced human sensory system as a prerequisite to human consciousness. See Peter Selg: *Vom Logos menschlicher Physis. Die Entfaltung einer anthroposophischen Humanphysiologie im Werk Rudolf Steiners*. Dornach 2000, pp. 262ff. In this overall context, Rudolf Steiner's presentation in Munich on August 25, 1918, should also be noted. There, with reference to his lectures in Prague on March 23 and 24, 1911 (GA 128), and in anticipation of his lecture in Basel on October 1, 1911, Rudolf Steiner described the upward etheric flow from the heart to the brain as the prerequisite to human perception and thought activity, which relate to the world and are thus have the potential for selflessness and transcending the body (See Selg: *Vom Logos menschlicher Physis*, pp. 226ff.).

20 Selg: *Vom Logos menschlicher Physis*, pp. 277ff.

21 "To behold the real, true 'I' we must first lose the earthly 'I.' It is impossible to approach the true 'I' without developing this devotion. We might say that in order to appear or reveal itself, the true 'I' cannot be sought; it hides when we look for it. It is found only in love, and love is our own being's devotion to a foreign being. That is why the true 'I' must be discovered like a foreign being" (84, 142).

22 At present, we human beings are capable of transforming thoughts into vibrations in the air by using our respiratory organs as organs of speech. We imprint our inner experiences on the outer world by transforming them into vibrations in the air, which reproduce what is happening inside us. In future, we will become increasingly able to externalize our own inner being in this way, and the end result will be that we will use our completely perfected organs of speech to bring forth our own kind; that is, to reproduce ourselves.

Our organs of speech, therefore, have the potential to become organs of reproduction in the future" (11, 177ff.).

23   The active Christ Impulse is clearly relevant to selflessness, death, and resurrection in the sensory sphere (see Selg: *Vom Logos menschlicher Physis*, pp. 262ff), to enabling true I-cognition, and to reproduction through the Word in the spiritual-scientific sense. With regard to spiritually understanding the sense of "I," however, we should also be aware that Rudolf Steiner described the human form in its entirety as the organ of this sensory activity: "The organ of perception for the 'I' of other human beings is the human form at rest, centered on the head." (170, 242) In Pforzheim on March 7, 1914, Rudolf Steiner spoke about the third preliminary stage of the Mystery of Golgotha, expanding on his treatment of the subject in Copenhagen in June 1911: "As a consequence [of the Nathan being becoming imbued by the Christ Being for the third time] during the ancient Lemurian period (but in etheric, spiritual heights), the future Nathan Jesus, who would otherwise have retained the form of an angel, assumed human form—etherically, of course, not in the flesh. At that time, the etheric angelic figure of Jesus of Nazareth existed in the closest region above the earth. When permeated by the Christ, he assumed the etheric form of a human being. Something new penetrated the cosmos, something that is now radiating out over the earth, making it possible for the physical, earthly human form (into which the strength of the etheric, supraearthly Christ Being flowed) to protect itself from the destruction that would have set in if the formative force that allows it to become an upright being had not streamed into it from the cosmos (152, 106).

24   In 1922, in an essay on the human "I," Rudolf Steiner wrote: "Initially, we apply the word 'I' to the unique coloration of soul experiences in ordinary consciousness, but without any understanding of what this word expresses. We acquire this understanding gradually as inner vision teaches us how the I-experience relates to our other inner experiences. We can observe how the experience of hunger in its early stages

relates to the experience of being satiated. We note that the
early stages of hunger intensify the I-feeling whereas the
experience of satiety subdues it; this is related to the urge to
rest after eating to satiety. The relationship changes in later
stages, when hunger begins to have destructive effects on
the organism. Continuing these observations, we note that
what the word 'I' denotes is not fulfillment on the soul level
but rather something like longing or desire. Thoughts we
entertain strengthen our feeling of being an 'I' only if they
are ideals; that is, if desire is inherent in them. Our ordinary
consciousness experiences the 'I' in the sphere of desires. On
this level, therefore, it is a longing for fulfillment, a source of
selfishness. We can also call the 'I' the 'night' of ordinary consciousness. The more we fill ourselves with thoughts of the
world, the more our experience of the 'I' retreats. To experience the 'I' strongly, we must first eliminate thoughts of the
world from our soul. These thoughts allow us to experience
our inner 'day,' whereas in the 'I,' we initially experience ourselves as if in an inner 'night.' Our inner day, however, does
not solve the riddle of the night; that requires a different
light. The 'I' longs for sunshine but is not satisfied by the
outer world's sunshine. The 'I' anticipates and desires sunshine. As Self, the 'I' demands fulfillment from selflessness. It
is always on the way to allowing the stream of selflessness to
emerge from the source of selfishness. ... Living in true moral
impulses is the beginning of experiencing the spirit world."
(36, 73ff.).

25 See the meeting of the upward-striving etheric bloodstream
with the "stream" of morality in the area of the pineal gland,
as described by Rudolf Steiner on October 1, 1911, op. cit.,
in Basel (130, 89ff.).

26 Re: Christ as the future "Lord of Karma," see in particular
Rudolf Steiner's lectures in Karlsruhe on October 7 and 14,
1911, (GA 131) and in Nuremberg on December 2, 1911,
(GA 130).

27 Inge Scholl: *Die weiße Rose*. 10th edition, Frankfurt 2003, p.
49.

28   "Das Geheimnis der Wunde. Aufzeichnungen zum Sam-
     ariterkurs." *Beiträge zur Rudolf Steiner Gesamtausgabe*, No.
     108, 1992, p. 8.
29   Ibid., p. 14.
30   Ibid., italics added.
31   Ibid., p. 46 (reproduced from the manuscript).
32   In a lecture to nurses in training at Herdecke Community
     Hospital, Gerhard Kienle spoke about Christ's words, "Love
     your neighbor as yourself": "Here is the challenge: to live
     with the terms of the other person's existence, which means
     extracting your own will, willing the other's existence,
     plunging into the other person's existential situation. This
     expansion of self—being one with the other person's exis-
     tence—is a recurrent motif throughout the New Testament.
     It means that a will-activity can appear in human beings that
     is capable not only of freeing itself from bodily nature (which
     would be pure asceticism), but also of immersing itself in
     the other person's existential situation. In other words, this
     will-activity extends beyond us as individuals. This is a very
     important point: Human will is meant to expand! And what
     happens when this expansion includes the other person and
     the spiritual element in that person, which comes from God?
     'When two or three are gathered together in my name, I am
     there with you.' This means that when two or three people
     are together and their will extends to the spiritual element
     in each other, they approach the sphere where the Other
     is present. That is the only way we can understand what it
     means when Christ says, 'I will be with you always, even
     unto the end of time.' It means extension of the will beyond
     the personal." (Gerhard Kienle: *Christentum und Medizin*.
     Stuttgart 1986, p. 61. For more information on Kienle, see
     Peter Selg: *Gerhard Kienle. Leben und Werk*. 2 volumes,
     Dornach 2003).
33   "Selflessness is the fundamental element in medicine." On
     Rudolf Steiner's soul-spiritual training in effective selflessness for
     therapists, see my studies *Krankheit und Christus-Erkenntnis.
     Anthroposophische Medizin als christliche Heilkunst*. 2nd

edition, Dornach 2003; and *Die Wärme-Meditation. Geschicht-licher Hintergrund und ideelle Beziehungen.* Dornach 2004. On Steiner's understanding of disease and therapy based on "insightful selflessness," see also my book *Krankheit, Schicksal und Heilung des Menschen. Über Rudolf Steiners geisteswissen-schaftliches Pathologie- und Therapieverständnis.* Dornach 2004.

34 See Peter Selg: *Der therapeutische Blick. Rudolf Steiner sieht Kinder.* Dornach 2005. [In English: *The Therapeutic Eye. How Rudolf Steiner Observed Children.* SteinerBooks: Great Barrington, MA 2008].

35 As quoted in Selg, *Der therapeutische Blick.*, p. 82. In English: *The Therapeutic Eye,* op. cit. note 34.

36 The version of this mantra published in 1999 in GA 268 (p. 310) by the Rudolf Steiner Archive was based on a copy. Meanwhile, it has been corrected in several places based on Steiner's original handwritten version, which was discovered among Ita Wegman's papers after her death.

37 See (among others) Ernst Klee: *"Euthanasie" im NS-Staat. Die "Vernichtung lebensunwerten Lebens."* Frankfurt 1985; Klee: *Auschwitz, die NS-Medizin und ihre Opfer.* Frankfurt 1997; Fridolf Kundlien: *Ärzte im Nationalsozialismus.* Cologne 1985. Robert Jay Lifton: *The Nazi Doctors.* New York 1987. As early as the beginning of the nineteenth century, ominous spiritual developments had begun to emerge. (See Selg: *Friedrich Schiller. Die Geistigkeit des Willens.* Dornach 2005, pp. 294ff and 263ff.) One year after Schiller's death, Christoph Wilhelm von Hufeland warned, "[Physicians] must and may not do anything other than pre-serve life. Whether that life is wanted or unwanted, valued or not valued, does not concern them. As soon as they pre-sume to incorporate such considerations into their practice, the consequences are incalculable and physicians become the most dangerous people in the nation. Once that line has been crossed and physicians believe themselves justified in deciding whether an individual life is necessary, it is simply a matter of incremental progression until the concept that an individual

human life lacks value and is therefore dispensable is applied in other instances." (As quoted in Gerhard Baader: "Heilen und Vernichten. Die Mentalität der NS-Ärzte." In: Angelika Ebbinghaus and Klaus Dörner, eds: *Vernichten und Heilen. Der Nürnberger Ärzteprozess und seine Folgen*. Berlin 2001, p. 278.)

38 Ernst Niekisch: *Das Reich der niederen Dämonen*. Hamburg 1953.

39 "Mysa stands beneath Mikael / transformed." See Emanuel Zeylmans van Emmichoven: *Die Erkraftung des Herzens. Rudolf Steiners Zusammenarbeit mit Ita Wegman*. Arlesheim 2009, p. 319.

40 See Emanuel Zeylmans van Emmichoven: *Wer war Ita Wegman? Eine Dokumentation*. 3 vols. Heidelberg 1990/92; and Selg: *"Ich bin für Fortschreiten." Ita Wegman und die Medizinische Sektion*. Dornach 2002. [In English: J.E. Zeylmans van Emmichoven: *Who was Ita Wegman. A Documentation*. 3 vols. Spring Valley, N.Y.: Mercury Press 1995/2005; and Selg: *I am for going ahead. Ita Wegman and the Medical Section*. Tr. Margot Saar. Great Barrington, MA: SteinerBooks 2012].

41 As quoted in Peter Selg: *Die letzten drei Jahre. Ita Wegman in Ascona. 1940-1943*. Dornach 2004, p. 44.

42 For details, see my monograph *Geistiger Widerstand und Überwindung. Ita Wegman 1993-1935*. Dornach 2005.

43 See Peter Selg: "Ita Wegmans soziale Wirksamkeit im 29. Jahrhundert." In: *Seelenpflege in Heilpädagogik und Sozialtherapie*. 4/2005, pp. 4-14.

44 As quoted in Selg: *Geistiger Widerstand und Überwindung*, p. 13.

45 Ibid., p. 22.

46 Ibid., p. 27.

47 Ibid., pp. 59 and 92.

48 See Selg: *Die letzten drei Jahre. Ita Wegman in Ascona. 1940-1943*, pp. 122ff; Emanuel Zeylmans van Emmichoven: *Wer war Ita Wegman? Eine Dokumentation*. Vol. 2, pp. 231ff. [In English: *Who was Ita Wegman. A Documentation*. Vol. 2.

Tr. Matthew Barton. Spring Valley, N.Y.: Mercury Press 2005; and Sergei O. Prokofieff: *The Occult Significance of Forgiveness*. Tr. Simon Blaxland de Lange. Forest Row, U.K: Temple Lodge 2004.

49 As quoted in Hans Müller-Wiedemann: *Karl König. Eine mitteleuropäische Biographie im 20. Jahrhundert*. Stuttgart 1992, p. 204.

50 As quoted in Selg: *Geistiger Widerstand und Überwindung*, pp. 155 and 157 (italics added).

51 See Peter Selg: *Karl König und die Anthroposophie. Zur Spiritualität eines esoterischen Christen im 20. Jahrhundert.* Dornach 2006 [*Karl König's Path into Anthroposophy*. Tr. Irene Czech. Floris Books: Edinburgh 2008].

52 "We noticed a certain change in our boy. He didn't want to wear any new clothes but always chose old items that we were going to give away. He said, 'I'm ashamed to walk around so well-dressed when I see so many people who are so poor.' It was difficult for us to know how to react. People we knew would come into our business and asked why we let our son walk around looking so shabby. 'After all, you're well off and can afford to buy clothes for him.' We simply said, 'That's how he wants it; there's nothing we can do about it.' In winter he often came home without his coat, and when we asked him where he had left it, he said, 'I saw a poor boy freezing because he had no coat, so I gave him mine.' Again and again he would ask, 'Why do we eat so well when other people are going hungry?' It was such a struggle to get him to eat a piece of good bread. I was filled with concern for him. ... His room was too fine for him. I gave him a generous allowance, and he always gave it away. He grew very withdrawn and uncommunicative, and we were very worried about him. We often went to the theater or to the coffee shop, but he never wanted to go with us. It's hard to describe how anxious we felt about coming home. He was filled with a sorrow that made it seem as if he had to bear all the pain of the world alone." (Bertha König, *Meine Kindheits- und Lebenserinnerungen*. Undated manuscript, pp. 56ff.).

53   As quoted in Müller-Wiedemann, op. cit., p. 21.

54   Ibid., p. 28.

55   See Hans Müller-Wiedemann's comprehensive descrip-
tion (note 49). Even today and even within the Camphill
Movement, its importance is still not adequately recognized.
In my opinion, in addition to being one of the greatest accom-
plishments of twentieth-century spiritual-scientific biography, it is also the product of the same forces that Müller-
Wiedemann writes about in such exemplary way. When
Müller-Wiedemann, then twenty-eight, arrived in Scotland
on March 30, 1953 (the twenty-eighth anniversary of Rudolf
Steiner's death), Karl König made a note in his diary about
their first meeting: "This afternoon I had a conversation with
Dr. Müller-Wiedemann, a student of Weizsäcker who has
now joined us. He is a refined and cultivated human being
who takes Romano Guardini as his role model, which is a
good thing." Scarcely five months later, König noted again,
"Had a long conversation with Dr. Müller-Wiedemann about
the community. I feel a very close connection to this young
physician" (Karl König Archive, Camphill).

56   On Karl König's empathy with the being of each handicapped
child he treated, see also Hans Müller-Wiedemann's description of the Camphill child conferences under König's direction: "In the early years, the participants experienced these
meetings as the core of König's mission to bring mystery-
based medicine to fruition. In penetrating the phenomena of
a child's biography, König's artistic vision consistently man-
aged to break through to the dimension of deeper karmic
realities and to use it as a basis for suggesting therapeutic
and curative educational approaches to benefit the child"
(op cit., p. 241). Note also the overall tone and style of Karl
König's lectures in Berlin on diagnostics in curative education (*Heilpädagogische Diagnostik*, Arlesheim 1983/84).
Moreover, Anke Weihs offers a remarkable account of a
patient's meeting with Karl König, comparable to how
Friedrich Rittelmeyer characterizes Rudolf Steiner (see in this
book, p. 44.): "I described the details to the medical assistant

in the little outer office. Then the door to the inner room opened. The last glow of the setting sun shone through the windows and filled the space. At the desk in the middle of the room sat a very small man with a large head, like a lion's. He wore a white physician's coat. His eyes were large and serious. When they rested on you, it was as if they not only saw through you but also created you anew. Something slumbering in you seemed to respond to this gaze; whether you wanted to or not, you seemed to become who you really were under all your layers of habits, inhibitions, and illusions. This particular gaze was one of Karl König's unique characteristics. I might call it his 'creative gaze.' He saw not only what you were, but also what you were charged with becoming. There are people who can observe and even see through others to the forces at work in them. Very few, however, have the gaze that creates anew. When we observe others, we can attempt to perceive the divine spark that lives in them. This inward approach becomes more successful through our anthroposophic efforts, but although it undoubtedly smoothes the way to the other person, it is not necessarily always associated with a stream of warmth, a living flow of communication. König's gaze, however, cut a channel for the flow of warmth. His very gaze had a healing effect, because you felt your most hidden truths were being recognized with empathy and respect. I think this first serious gaze (Dr. König said little) was the decisive step toward healing." (As quoted in Müller-Wiedemann, op. cit., pp. 101ff.).

57   Karl König: *Über das Wesen Camphills—drei Aspekte.* As quoted in Müller-Wiedemann, op. cit, pp. 202ff.

58   See Peter Selg: *Ita Wegman und Karl König. Eine biographische Documentation.* Dornach 2007. [In English: *Ita Wegman and Karl König. Letters and Documents.* Edinburgh: Floris Books 2009].

59   As quoted by Inge Scholl, op. cit., p. 126.

60   As quoted in: Inge Jens (ed.): *Hans Scholl und Sophie Scholl. Briefe und Aufzeichnungen.* 8th edition, Frankfurt 2003, p. 94.

61 As quoted by Inge Scholl, op. cit., p. 26.

62 Ibid., p. 89.

63 For more on the "voice of conscience" in the Christian tradition and in relationship to the coming of the etheric Christ and on the Christ Being's assumption of responsibility for the karmic order, see in this book pp. 16ff.; see also Karl König's fundamental explanations in *Die Mission des Gewissens* (Stuttgart 1992; lectures held in Föhrenbühl 1964/65).

64 As quoted in Inge Scholl, op. cit, pp. 90ff.

65 See Hans Scholl's Russian diary entries in: Inge Jens (ed.), op. cit., pp. 113-129.

66 As quoted in Inge Jens (ed.), op cit, p. 88.

67 The text of the flyer (which was written not by Hans Scholl, but by Professor Hans Huber) reads: "Germany's name will remain disgraced forever unless German young people finally stand up, expiating and avenging, smashing their tormenters and instituting a new spiritual Europe." (As quoted in Inge Scholl, op. cit., p. 95) Fourteen months earlier, in a letter to his friend Rose Nägele, Hans Scholl had described the actual Christological dimension of this "new spiritual Europe": *"For me, the birth of the Lord is the greatest possible religious experience, for he is born anew for me. In this light, Europe will have to be transformed, or it will perish!"* (Letter of December 30, 1941, as quoted in Inge Jens (ed.), op. cit, p. 322).

68 Inge Scholl, op. cit., p. 57.

69 Sophie Scholl's inner path, the basis for the decisiveness and certainty that her jailors found so incomprehensible, is outlined in her letters and diary entries: *"We all have our own inner standards, we just don't look for them enough. Perhaps because they are the most severe"* (May 16, 1940, as quoted in Inge Jens [ed.], op. cit., p. 177). Sophie Scholl's entire upbringing and adolescent development had fostered a radically ethical and religiously based self-image. As the war continued, she opted for the path of sacrifice for a "just cause" (May 22, 1940; ibid., p. 178) and accepted the consequences of her clear analysis of the situation: "I feel compelled to

outer actions that will manifest what until now has existed in me only as a thought, as an acknowledgement of what is right" (May 30, 1942; ibid., p 256). "I am often unhappy that all suffering cannot pass through me, because that would at least make amends for some of the guilt I feel toward the people whose suffering was undeserved and so much greater than mine.... You know the weight of a human life; we must know why we are throwing it into the balance" (January 3, 1943; ibid., p. 284). To her friend Lieutenant Fritz Hartnagel, who was fighting in Stalingrad, Sophie Scholl argued not only for the necessity of consistent, forceful pacifism but also for the spirit's victorious power of resurrection. Four months before her sacrificial death, which she accepted consciously as a consequence of her public actions, she pointed him emphatically toward the "glorious sentence" in Paul's Epistle to the Romans (Romans 8:2): "For the law of spirit, which brings life in Christ Jesus, has set me free from the law of sin and death" (October 28, 1942; ibid., p. 275). Given the Christological context of this volume, it should also be noted that at the beginning of Sophie Scholl's pivotal years in Munich, on January 2, 1942, she was deeply moved when Carl Muth showed her a picture of the image of Christ on the shroud of Turin. ("I have never seen anyone so deeply immersed in that big picture in the book I have than Sophie Scholl was today" (Muth, ibid., pp. 321ff.). After receiving a photograph of the shroud on January 20, 1942, she wrote to her brother Hans: "I am surprised that the picture hasn't caused more of a sensation. For a Christian, this is huge—it means seeing the face of God with our physical eyes. And it took technology to reveal this image!" (Ibid., p. 324). Hans Scholl himself was also deeply moved by photographic images of the shroud, which had been published in Germany in the late 1930s. At New Year's 1941/42, he sent the photographs to friends. His thoughts returned to the image again and again, and in an essay he wrote: "I have seen illustrations of what the Romans thought Christ looked like. How did I know without hesitation that He did not look like that? If

I see Christ as portrayed by Dürer or Giotto or El Greco, I
know immediately that these images are much closer to the
real Christ. And the strange thing is that all of these pictures
by the great masters are similar in their essential traits, and
all of them resemble this photograpic image. But in the case
of the image of the Shroud of Turin, the mysterious accord in
our hearts that allows us to experience an image as the real
Jesus is enhanced to the highest possible perfection that we
seek, but can never completely achieve in our desire to behold
the Christ.... Claudel speaks of the "second resurrection" of
Christ for the twentieth century. For nearly two thousand
years, this image of the Son of God has remained invisible,
sleeping and waiting for the spell to be broken. Beholding the
reality was reserved for our time." (Ibid., pp. 90ff.).

70   As reported by a guard, quoted in Inge Scholl, op. cit., p. 64.

71   As quoted by Inge Scholl, op. cit., p. 63.

72   Ibid., p. 49.

73   See also the study by Sergei O. Prokofieff: *The Encounter
with Evil and Its Overcoming through Spiritual Science,
with Essays on the Foundation Stone.* Tr. Simon Blaxland de
Lange. London: Temple Lodge 1999.

74   *Erinnerungen von Marie Steiner. Aufsätze und Gedichte.* Vol.
1. Dornach 1949, p. 9.

75   For example, in a newspaper article written in the spring of
1900, Rudolf Steiner writes pointedly, "I am filled with profound mistrust of individuals who talk a great deal about
selflessness or altruism. It seems to me that these people in
particular have no real sense of the egotistical comfort that
a selfless action confers.... Let us dispense with the lie, as if
there were any such thing as relinquishing self or selflessness
for its own sake. There are indeed selfless individuals who
spend their lives in devoted love. But it is not true that they
give up selfhood. They love because love offers the greatest
possible self-indulgence; they love because they delight in
giving of themselves." (30, 429/431).

76   As quoted in Peter Selg: *Vom Logos menschlicher Physis*, pp.
51ff.

77 See in this context works by Sergei O. Prokofieff: *Rudolf Steiner and the Founding of the New Mysteries*. Tr. Paul King and Simon Blaxland de Lange. London: Temple Lodge 1994 and *May Human Beings Hear It!* op. cit. note 18.

78 Friedrich Rittelmeyer: *Mein Lebensbegegnung mit Rudolf Steiner*. 10th edition, Stuttgart 1983, p. 35. [In English: *Rudolf Steiner Enters My Life*. Tr. D. S. Osmond. Floris Books: Edinburgh 1963].

79 Belyi, op. cit., p. 444.

80 Ibid., pp. 438ff.

81 As quoted in Peter Selg: *Rudolf Steiner und das Fünfte Evangelium*, p. 125. [In English: *Rudolf Steiner and the Fifth Gospel*. Tr. Catherine E. Creeger. SteinerBooks 2010].

82 Belyi, op. cit., p. 491.

83 See Peter Selg: *Rudolf Steiner und das Fünfte Evangelium*, pp. 117ff. [In English: *Rudolf Steiner and the Fifth Gospel*, op. cit. note 81].

84 Rudolf Steiner's unambiguous statement, that *he* would lead the Sections *through* the Section heads (260, pp. 143ff, specifically with regard to Marie Steiner, Ita Wegman, and Edith Maryon), which came only 15 months before his death, when he was already aware that his remaining time was very limited, was telling evidence that his concept of leadership consciously extended into the time after death. In fact, this statement assumes the independent posthumous continuation of his existing esoteric collaboration with each earthly Section head.

85 As quoted in Selg, *Rudolf Steiner und das Fünfte Evangelium*, pp. 10ff. [In English: *Rudolf Steiner and the Fifth Gospel*, op. cit. note 81].

86 See Sergei O. Prokofieff: *Die Grundsteinmeditation. Ein Weg zu den neuen christlichen Mysterien*, p. 91. [In English: *The Foundation Stone Meditation: A Key to the Christian Mysteries*. Tr. Maria St. Goar. London: Temple Lodge 2007].

87 First published in: *Natura. Eine Zeitschrift zur Erweiterung der Heilkunst nach geisteswissenschaftlicher Menschenkunde.* Vol. 4, 1929/30, pp. 1-6.

Bibliography

GA 2   *Goethe's Theory of Knowledge: An Outline of the Epistemology of His Worldview.* Tr. Peter Clemm. Great Barrington, MA: SteinerBooks 2008. In German: *Grundlinien einer Erkenntnistheorie der Goetheschen Weltanschauung, mit besonderer Rücksicht auf Schiller.*

GA 9   *Theosophy: An Introduction to the Spiritual Processes in Human Life and in the Cosmos.* Tr. Catherine E. Creeger. Great Barrington, MA: SteinerBooks 1994. In German: *Theosophie. Einführung in übersinnliche Welterkenntnis und Menschenbestimmung.*

GA 11   *Cosmic Memory.* Tr. Karl E. Zimmer. Great Barrington, MA: SteinerBooks 2006. In German: *Aus der Akasha-Chronik.*

GA 12   *The Stages of Higher Knowledge: Imagination, Inspiration, Intuition.* In German: *Die Stufen der höheren Erkenntnis.*

GA 17   *The Threshold of the Spiritual World.* See *A Way of Self-Knowledge.* Tr. Christopher Bamford. Great Barrington, MA: SteinerBooks 2006. In German: *Die Schwelle der geistigen Welt: Aphoristische Ausführungen.*

GA 26   *Anthroposophical Leading Thoughts.* Tr. George and Mary Adams. Forest Row, England: Rudolf Steiner Press 1998. In German: *Anthroposophische Leitsätze.*

GA 30   *Individualism in Philosophy.* Tr. William Lindeman. Spring Valley, NY: Mercury Press 2007. In German: *Methodische Grundlagen der Anthroposophie: Gesmmelte Aufsätze zur Philosophie, Naturwissenschaft, Ästhetik und Seelenkunde 1884-1901).*

GA 36   *Der Goetheanumgedanke inmitten der Kulturkrisis der Gegenwart* [The Goetheanum-idea in the middle of the present cultural crisis] (1921-1925): 1st edition 1961.

GA 39   *Briefe Band II* (1890-1925) [*Letters. Vol. 2. 1890-1925*]: 2nd edition 1987.

GA 84   *Was wollte das Goetheanum und was soll die Anthroposophie?* [What Was the Intention of the Goetheanum and Anthroposophy? Lectures to Members of the Anthroposophical Society] (1923/24): 2nd edition 1989.

GA 93   *The Temple Legend: Freemasonry and Related Occult Movements: From the Contents of the Esoteric School.* Forest Row, U.K. Rudolf Steiner Press 2002. In German: *Die Tempellegende und die Goldene Legende.*

GA 96   *Original Impulses for the Science of the Spirit.* Tr. Anna Meuss. Lower Beechmont, Australia: Completion Press. In German: *Ursprungsimpulse der Geisteswissenschaft. Christliche Esoterik im Lichte neuer Geist-Erkenntnis.*

GA 99   *Rosicrucian Wisdom.* Tr. revised J. Collis. Forest Row, England: Rudolf Steiner Press 2000. (Previously published as *Theosophy of the Rosicrucian*). In German: *Die Theosophie des Rosenkreuzers.*

GA 109   *The Principle of Spiritual Economy.* Tr. Peter Mollenhauer. Hudson, N.Y.: Anthroposophic Press 1986. In German: *Das Prinzip der spirituellen Ökonomie im Zusammenhang mit Wiederverkörperungsfragen.*

GA 116   *Der Christus-Impulse und die Entwicklung des Ich-Bewusstseins* [The Christ Impulse and the Development of "I" Consciousness] (1909/10): 4th edition 1982.

GA 118   *Das Ereignis der Christus-Erscheinung in der ätherischen Welt.* (See *The Reappearance of Christ in the Etheric.* Great Barrington, MA: SteinerBooks 2003).

GA 128   *An Occult Physiology.* Facsimilie of 3rd revised edition of 1983. Tr. unknown. Forest Row, U.K.: Rudolf Steiner Press 2005. In german: *Eine okkulte Physiologie.*

GA 130   *Esoteric Christianity and the Mission of Christian Rosenkreutz.* Rev. tr. Matthew Barton. London: Rudolf Steiner Press 2005. In German: *Das esoterische Christentum und die geistige Führung des Menschen.*

GA 131   *From Jesus to Christ.* Forest Row, U.K.: Rudolf Steiner Press 2005. In German: *Von Jesus zu Christus.*

GA 133   *Earthly and Cosmic Man.* Blauvelt, NY: Garber Communications 1986. In German: *Der irdische und der kosmische Mensch.*

GA 142   *The Bhagavad Gita and the West: The Esoteric Significance of the Bhagavad Gita and Its Relation to the Epistles of Paul*. Great Barrington, MA: SteinerBooks 2009. In German: *Die Bhagavad Gita und die Paulusbriefe*.

GA 143   *Erfahrungen des Übersinnlichen* [Experiences of the suprasensory] (1912): 4th edition 1994.

GA 148   *The Fifth Gospel: From the Akashic Chronicle*. Tr. Anna Meuss. Forest Row, U.K.: Rudolf Steiner Press 1998. In German: *Aus der Akasha-Forschung. Das Fünfte Evangelium*.

GA 149   *Christ and the Spiritual World: And the Search for the Holy Grail*. Tr. C. Davy and D.S. Osmond. Forest Row, U.K.: Rudolf Steiner Press 2008. In German: *Christus und die geistigen Welt. Von der Suche nach dem heiligen Gral*.

GA 152   *Approaching the Mystery of Golgotha*. Tr. Michael Miller. Great Barrington, MA: SteinerBooks 2006. In German: *Vorstufen zum Mysterium von Golgatha*.

GA 155   *Christ and the Human Soul*. Tr. C. Davy and M. Cotterell. Forest Row, U.K.: Rudolf Steiner Press 2008. In German: *Christus und die menschliche Seele. Uber den Sinn des Lebens. Theosophische Moral. Anthroposophie und Christentum*.

GA 158   *Der Zusammenhang des Menschen mit der elementarischen Welt. Kalawala—Olaf Asteson—Das russische Volkstum— Die Welt als Ergebnis von Gleichgewichtswirkungen* [The connection between human beings and the elemental world: The Kalavala, Olaf Asteson—the Russian people—the world as a result of the effects of equilibrium]: 3rd edition 1990.

GA 168   *The Connection between the Living and the Dead*. Tr. Aria Jackson. Great Barrington, MA: SteinerBooks 2012. In German: *Die Verbindung zwischen Lebenden und Toten*.

GA 170   *The Riddle of Humanity. The Spiritual Background of Human History*. London: Rudolf Steiner Press 1990. In German: *Das Rätsel des Menschen. Die geistigen Hintergründe der menschlichen Geschichte*.

GA 175   *Building Stones for an Understanding of the Mystery of Golgotha*. Tr. A.H. Parker. London: Rudolf Steiner Press

1985. In German: *Bausteine zu einer Erkenntnis des Mysteriums von Golgatha.*

GA 185   *From Symptom to Reality in Modern History.* Tr. A.H. Parker. London: Rudolf Steiner Press 1976. In German: *Geschichliche Symptomatologie.*

GA 188   *Der Goetheanismus—ein Umwandlungsimpuls und Auferstehungsgedanke. Menschenwissenschaft und Sozialwissenschaft* [Goetheanism, an impulse for transformation and thought of resurrection: human science and social science] (1919): 3rd edition 1982.

GA 194   *Die Sendung Michaels.* See *The Archangel Michael.* Tr. Marjorie Spock. Great Barrington, MA: SteinerBooks/ Anthroposophic Press 1994.

GA 198   *Heilfaktoren für den sozialen Organismus* [Healing factors for the social organism] (1920): 2nd edition 1984.

GA 218   *Geistige Zusammenhänge in der Gestaltung des menschlichen Organismus* [Spiritual Connections in the formation of the human organism} (1922): 3rd edition 1992. See the first 2 lectures in *Waldorf Education and Anthroposophy Vol. 2* Public lectures 1922-1924. Hudson, N.Y.: Anthroposophic Press 1996.

GA 220   *Lebendiges Naturerkennen. Intellektueller Sündenfall und spirituelle Sündenerhebung* [Living knowledge of nature: intellectual fall of humankind] (1923): 2nd edition 1982.

GA 223   See *The Cycle of the Year as Breathing Process of the Earth.* Tr. Barbara D. Betteridge and Frances E. Dawson. Great Barrington, MA: Anthroposophic Press/ SteinerBooks 1984. See also *Michaelmas and the Soul-Forces of Man.* Tr. Samuel and Loni Lockwood. Great Barrington, MA: SteinerBooks 1946, 2012. In German: *Der Jahreskreislauf als Atmungsvorgang der Erde und die vier grossen Festeszeiten.*

GA 260   *The Christmas Conference for the Foundation of the General Anthroposophical Society 1923/1924.* Tr. Johanna Collis. Hudson, NY: Anthroposophic Press/ SteinerBooks 1990. In German: *Die Weihnachtstagung zur Begründung der Allgemeinen Anthroposophischen Gesellschaft. 1923/24.*

GA 260a *The Foundation Stone. The Life, Nature and Cultivation of Anthroposophy.* London: Rudolf Steiner Press 1996. In German: *Die Konstitution der Allgemeinen Anthroposophischen Gesellschaft und der Freien Hochschule für Geisteswissenschaft.*

GA 262 *Correspondence and Documents. 1901-1925.* Tr. Christian and Ingrid von Arnim. Hudson, NY: Anthroposophic Press 1988. In German: *Rudolf Steiner/Marie Steiner-von Sivers: Briefwechsel und Dokumente (1901-1925).*

GA 268 *Mantrische. Sprüche. Seelenübungen II. 1903–1925.* [In English: Soul Exercises. Vol 2. Mantric Verses 1903-1925].

GA 316 *A Course for Young Doctors.* Spring Valley, NY: Mercury Press. In German: *Meditative Betrachtungen und Anleitungen zur Vertiefung der Heilkunst.*

GA 343 *Vorträge und Kurse über christlich-religiöses Wirken, II* [Lectures and courses on Christian religious work. Vol. 2] (1921): 1st edition 1993.

GA 346 *The Book of Revelation and the Work of the Priest.* Tr. J. Collis. Forest Row, U.K.: Rudolf Steiner Press 2001. In German: *Vorträge und Kurse über christlich-religiöses Wirken, Bd. 5, Apokalypse und Priesterwirken.*

THE PATH OF THE SOUL AFTER DEATH: *The Community of the Living and the Dead as Witnessed by Rudolf Steiner in his Eulogies and Farewell Addresses* (2010)

RUDOLF STEINER'S INTENTIONS FOR THE ANTHROPOSOPHICAL SOCIETY: *The Executive Council, the School for Spiritual Science, and the Sections* (2011)

On Anthroposophical Medicine and Curative Education:

I AM FOR GOING AHEAD: *Ita Wegman's Work for the Social Ideals of Anthroposophy* (2012)

KARL KÖNIG: THE CHILD WITH SPECIAL NEEDS: *Letters and Essays on Curative Education* (Ed.) (2009).

ITA WEGMAN AND KARL KÖNIG: *Letters and Documents* (2009)

KARL KÖNIG: MY TASK: *Autobiography and Biographies* (Ed.) (2008)

KARL KÖNIG'S PATH TO ANTHROPOSOPHY (2008)

On Child Development and Waldorf Education:

I AM DIFFERENT FROM YOU: *How Children Experience Themselves and the World in the Middle of Childhood* (2011)

THE ESSENCE OF WALDORF EDUCATION (2010)

UNBORNNESS: *Human Pre-existence and the Journey toward Birth* (2010)

A GRAND METAMORPHOSIS: *Contributions to the Spiritual-Scientific Anthropology and Education of Adolescents* (2008)

THE THERAPEUTIC EYE: *How Rudolf Steiner Observed Children* (2008)

Ita Wegman Institute
for Basic Research into Anthroposophy

Pfeffinger Weg 1 A CH-4144 Arlesheim, Switzerland
www.wegmaninstitut.ch
e-mail: sekretariat@wegmaninstitut.ch

The Ita Wegman Institute for Basic Research into Anthroposophy is a non-profit research and teaching organization. It undertakes basic research into the lifework of Dr. Rudolf Steiner (1861–1925) and the application of Anthroposophy in specific areas of life, especially medicine, education, and curative education. The Institute also contains and cares for the literary estates of Ita Wegman, Madeleine van Deventer, Hilma Walter, Willem Zeylmans van Emmichoven, Karl Schubert, and others. Work carried out by the Institute is supported by a number of foundations and organizations and an international group of friends and supporters. The Director of the Institute is Prof. Dr. Peter Selg.

CPSIA information can be obtained
at www.ICGtesting.com
Printed in the USA
BVHW070935060222
628142BV00001B/96